D0522160

# TRUTH
# AND OPINION

# TRUTH
# AND OPINION.

*Historical Essays*

BY

## C. V. WEDGWOOD

COLLINS
ST JAMES'S PLACE, LONDON
1960

*TO*
# G. M. YOUNG

# Acknowledgments

I am indebted to the Cambridge University Press for permission to re-print my Leslie Stephen Lecture, *The Sense of the Past*; to the Leicester University Press for permission to re-print my Fairclough Lecture, *The Common Man in the Great Civil War*; to Messrs. Longman's for *Social Comedy in the Reign of Charles I* which first appeared in *Studies in Social History: a tribute to G. M. Trevelyan*, edited by J. H. Plumb; to Arthur Barker for *The Last Masque* which appeared in *The Book of the P.E.N.*; to Andre Deutsch and *Time and Tide* for *Captain Hind the Highwayman* which was included in the *Time and Tide Anthology* edited by Anthony Lejeune; to the editor of the *Times Literary Supplement* for *Machiavell.* and the editors of *History To-day* for *The Causes of the English Civil War*; to the Royal Historical Society, The English Association, the Royal Society of Literature, the PEN Club and the Glasgow branch of the University Women's Association for permission to use lectures originally given at their invitation: *Scots and English 1603-1640; Literature and the Historian; Art, Truth and History; History and Imagination; Principles and Perspectives;* also to the *London Magazine* which published *Art, Truth and History*; and to the British Council for whom the essay on *Edward Gibbon* was originally written. The Introduction to this volume incorporates some paragraphs from an article written for *The Craft of Letters in England* edited by John Lehmann for the Cresset Press, to whom I am indebted for permission to use the material. I am also grateful to the authors and publishers for permission to quote extracts from the following works: *History of the English Speaking Peoples* by Sir Winston Churchill, Cassell; *Queen Victoria* by Lytton Strachey, Chatto and Windus; *English Social History* by G. M. Trevelyan, Longmans, Green & Co.; *The Common Reader* by Virginia Woolf, Leonard Woolf. I would also like to thank Miss Poly Marczali and Miss Catherine Hoare for help in putting this collection together and preparing it for the press.

C. V. W.

# Contents

*It is not truth but opinion that can travel
the world without a passport*
SIR WALTER RALEIGH

# Introduction

THE QUOTATION from Sir Walter Raleigh which provides the
title for this collection of essays may seem an unduly defeatist
maxim for a historian, as though there were no possibility of
establishing, let alone of propagating, the truth. It is not as
pessimistic as it sounds for some opinions are closer to truth
than others and the historian lives in the hope that his work
may lead to a closer connection between them.

Several of the essays in this book deal directly with ways of
approaching the truth and ways of communicating it. Some of
them deal with the problem of morality in history, and some
with scenes, incidents and arguments from the past. For twenty-
five years I have been looking for a philosophy of history without
finding one in which I could believe, either in the works of
philosopher historians ancient and modern, or by my own
meditations. But in the last years it has seemed to me that the
practice of writing history, pursued certainly with passion and
I hope with honesty, can produce if not a philosophy, at least a
point of view clear enough to give purpose and perspective to
what is written.

My writing experience has led me to set a very high value
on investigating *what* men did and *how* things happened. Pieces
like *The Last Masque* and *Captain Hind the Highwayman* were
written partly to provide entertainment; they are small literary
diversions. But they were also written because limited and

relatively simple subjects like these, where passion and prejudices play little part, give the historian an opportunity for the purest kind of enquiry. The apparent objectives may seem light and even frivolous, but the experiment in reconstructing as accurately and fully as possible a detached incident or a character *without attempting to prove any general point or demonstrate any theory whatsoever* is a useful exercise. I have found by experience that in the course of such neutral enquiries unexpected clues are found to far more important matters. *The Last Masque* gave me numerous indications for lines of enquiry into the Court and administration of Charles I and *Captain Hind* has left me with a handful of hints, ideas and sources for the social consequences of the Civil War.

The older historians concentrated more on narrative than on analysis, on the *How* rather than the *Why* of history. But now, for several generations, *Why* has been regarded as a more important question than *How*. It is, of course, a more important question. But it cannot be answered until *How* is established. The careful, thorough and accurate answer to the question *How* should take the historian a long way towards answering the question *Why*; but for this purpose narrative history must be written with depth and reflection, thought through stage by stage, and recorded comprehensively and with unremitting attention to chronology. As long as this narrative aspect of history is neglected, as long as the *How* is imperfectly apprehended, the answers given to the question *Why* will be imperfect. There will be (indeed, there is) much learned putting of carts before horses and offering of abstruse explanations for sequences of events which present no problem at all if the historic landscape is looked at as a whole and not divided into unnatural sections. No development in history is self-contained or self-explanatory, and though specialization is essential for learning it is fatal to understanding. General history stands both at the beginning and at the end of all the questions.

I have been told that to write only of how things happened is to abdicate the historian's function, which should be to draw conclusions and explain processes. But are we to presume that no one but ourselves is capable of making deductions from facts? Must the historian, like an old-fashioned writer for the young, be for ever pointing out the lesson as well as telling the story? Is not the intelligent reader of history, like the intelligent reader of poetry or novels, able to take the points for himself, without underlining, repetition, and summing up? "Work it out for yourself" is the tacit message of most creative writers to their readers. Why then should the historian assume that his readers alone have too little imagination, perception and responsive power to take the challenge? I cannot feel that it is the function of the historian to do all the thinking for his public. If history is educational—and I have a vested interest in believing it to be so—it must be an education in thinking not merely in remembering.

An interest in how things happened and a great desire to find out does not make a philosophy of history. But the quest for facts, past or present, provides some experience for a philosophy of life. These essays mark a few of the stages, the halts and the recreations on a journey towards that always retreating horizon where truth and opinion meet.

*London,* 1959

# PART I

## ART, TRUTH AND HISTORY

# THE SENSE OF THE PAST

RALPH PENDEREL, the hero of that tantalizingly un-finished fragment by Henry James, *The Sense of the Past*, had written—it was his only literary achievement—an unpre-tending work called *An Essay in aid of the Reading of History*. From all we ever hear of this work it sounds a not very original consideration of the magic of old places and old things, redeemed by the extraordinary intensity with which its author experienced a relatively commonplace romantic emotion. 'There are par-ticular places,' Ralph Penderel is supposed to have written, ' where things have happened, places enclosed and ordered and subject to the continuity of life mostly, that seem to put us into communication, and the spell is sometimes made to work by the imposition of hands, if it be patient enough, on an old object or an old surface.' There is nothing very remarkable in the sentiment, but we are asked to believe that Ralph Penderel's attachment to the past, or rather to surviving objects of the past, was a faith strong enough to work a miracle, and transfer him back a century in time.

Even in fiction such miracles are to be distrusted, although the surviving pages of *The Sense of the Past* suggest that Henry James would have explored the impossible situation with a rare subtlety. But I have pirated his title because it indicates the nature of a problem, part historical, part literary, which has increasingly concerned students of the past. Is there anything

19

to be said for the cultivation of the sense of the past, for the attempt to make the imaginative leap from our own epoch to an earlier one? Is it helpful to serious historical inquiry to encourage some play of the imagination; is it a dangerous folly or an essential exercise? The frontier between scholarship and creative literature is a disputed one, over which there has been much verbal combat. In this particular problem, that of historical imagination, literature has made significant contributions to scholarship and scholarship to literature.

We learn from the preface of the first edition to Henry James's posthumous fragment *The Sense of the Past* that he turned to this historical ghost story partly to take his mind off the troubles of the contemporary world during the First World War. His hero, too, found in the contemplation of the past a relief from the difficulties of the present. The desire for withdrawal, admitted or not, is often a powerful motive in driving the student, whether he be an amateur or a professional, towards the study of history. This element of escape implies also a certain lack of realism, which easily becomes a desire to idealize or at least to romanticize the past. The serious student of history, if he has, or is aware of, this weakness, has to be constantly on guard against it. On the other hand without this romantic impetus, without this desire to remove from one age into another, to imagine and to share in the thoughts and feelings of a time remote from the present, historical inquiry would lack an essential element. Historical knowledge is in debt to the romantic writers, not so much for what they themselves did (though some of them made considerable advances in the study of the past), as for the deeper and wider scope that they gave to historical inquiry.

The summoning up of emotion like that of Henry James's hero, over some particular object or some particular place, hallowed by some great or supposedly great event, was not of course peculiar to the romantic or post romantic epoch. Cicero spoke of ' the power of admonition that is in places '. Montaigne pondered on this way of feeling, in the sixteenth century: 'Is it nature, or by some error of fantasy, that the seeing of places that we know to have been frequented or inhabited by men whose memory is esteemed or mentioned in stories doth in some sort move and stir us up as much or more than hearing their noble deeds.'

Even the unsentimental Gibbon who was not, as he himself said, ' very susceptible of enthusiasm,' was moved in this way by his first visit to Rome. ' After a sleepless night, I trod with a lofty step the ruins of the Forum. Each memorable spot where Romulus stood, or Tully spoke, or Cæsar fell, was at once present to my eye, and several days of intoxication were lost or enjoyed before I could descend to a cool or minute investigation.' But that ' cool or minute investigation ' was the proper occupation of an inhabitant of the age of Reason, and Gibbon took care to let the intoxication evaporate before he began on the serious business of inquiry. To judge by this passage, he was also doubtful if these days of intoxication, which he admits he enjoyed, were not, by a more severe judgment, to be accounted ' lost.'

Dr. Johnson, on the other hand, did not hesitate to ascribe some value to these intoxicating emotions. ' Far from me and from my friends be such frigid philosophy as may conduct us indifferent and unmoved over any ground which has been dignified by wisdom, bravery or virtue. That man is little to be envied whose patriotism would not gain force upon the plain of Marathon or whose piety would not grow warmer among the ruins of Iona.' This is already very close indeed to the frankly romantic fervour of John Keats:

21

*There is a charm in footing slow across the silent plain*
*Where patriot battle has been fought, where glory had the gain;*
*There is a pleasure in the heath where Druids old have been*
*Where mantles grey have rustled by and swept the nettled green . . .*

Clearly the feelings experienced, or manufactured, by Johnson, by Keats, and by many others, owed much less to knowledge of the past than they did to modern emotions; they were using historic sites not to strengthen their vision of the past for its own intrinsic interest, but simply to heighten their contemporary sensations of patriotism or piety. This is a very common and often enough, in literature, an effective use of history. It is clearly seen in Wordsworth's sonnet inspired by seeing the site of the victory of Dundee's Highlanders at Killiecrankie in 1689. The title underlines the point: ' In the pass of Killiecrankie, an invasion being expected, October 1803.' Dorothy Wordsworth, in her account of the Highland tour undertaken in that year, records that she and her brother, walking above the river Garry in the pass of Killiecrankie, spoke of the impending invasion; the thought of one deed of arms had instantly and naturally suggested the threat under which they were living. A story in Scott's Border Minstrelsy seems to have touched off the poem itself. A veteran Highland soldier at the battle of Sheriffmuir, maddened by the vacillations of the Jacobite commander, said, ' Oh for one hour of Dundee '. Wordsworth in 1803 echoes the wish:

*Oh, for a single hour of that Dundee*
*Who on that day the word of onset gave!*
*Like conquest would the men of England see;*
*And her foes find a like inglorious grave.*

The feeling behind the Killiecrankie sonnet is one of contemporary hope and anxiety, merely heightened by reference to a past which is itself very imperfectly realized. Such lines as

> *And Garry thundering down her mountain road*
> *Was stopped and could not breathe beneath the load*
> *Of the dead bodies*

do not convey the impression that the poet saw what actually happened at Killiecrankie in any but theatrical terms. He makes the river human, but forgets that the men were.

This use of the past merely to heighten a modern effect is permissible in certain contexts, or at least to writers of commanding stature. But it was a common romantic vice to encourage a purely theatrical view of the past, as though history were an opera house inhabited by puppets striking noble attitudes preferably in picturesque settings, and quite removed from the ordinary embarrassments and distresses of mortal life. The facile muse of Mrs. Hemans ran riot in this fashion when she turned her attention to the persecution of the Vaudois among Alpine scenery of great grandeur:

> *Go, if thou lovest the soil to tread*
> *Where man hath nobly striven,*
> *And life, like incense, hath been shed,*
> *An offering unto Heaven.*
>
> *Far o'er the snows and round the pines,*
> *Hath swept a noble flood;*
> *The nurture of the peasants' vines*
> *Hath been the martyrs' blood. . .*

and so on for any number of verses.

She had only to consider any factual account of religious, or any other, persecution to know that human life is not shed like incense. She had only to look into Milton's sonnet ' On the Late Massacre in Piedmont ' and ponder nine words of it— ' whose bones lie scattered on the Alpine mountains cold '—and shudder at that, before tinkling on about men and women whose lives and deaths she had made not the slightest effort either to understand or imagine. Mrs. Hemans's verses belong very much to her own time, but her type of sentimental historical fantasy is the worst legacy of the romantics and is still with us in other forms today. As a way of thinking about the past, it is devoid of any real curiosity about it, and springs merely from the desire to stimulate a flattering emotion or a vicarious thrill. It is the outlook of those ghoulishly concerned only with disaster, for whom no castle is complete without dungeons and *oubliette*, no ancient house without its priests' hole and secret panel, and who greedily lap up whatever nonsense has been invented about the alleged bloodstains on the floor.

But place has a real as well as a spurious charm and the more serious student of history does often find fascination in visiting the site of an event, quite apart from the value as evidence which it may also possess. The charm exercised by objects can be equally powerful. There is a fascination in the continued physical existence of chairs, tables, spoons, goblets, trenchers—things that were used and handled, not necessarily by the rare and famous whose names have survived, but simply by some of the millions whose names are as dead and forgotten as they are themselves.

The massive editing of documents over the last century, and the increasing use of such modern aids to research as photostat and microfilm, have relieved the historian of the continual necessity of manuscript research, though there will always remain certain things about which the manuscript and the manuscript only can enlighten us. But it is not necessity alone which draws the

student of history constantly back to manuscript documents.
There is a peculiar pleasure in the mere contact of the hand
with the paper. I can speak with assurance only for that epoch
to which most of my manuscript researches have been confined,
the seventeenth century. Nothing seems to bridge the gap of
the years so much as the unfolding and reading of ancient letters;
sometimes minute particles of sand which had long adhered in
some thick down stroke where the ink had been wet, detach
themselves after three hundred years to blow away and join with
yesterday's dust. This feeling for objects not merely as evidence
but *for themselves* is not logically defensible; the moment we
think about it we see that they do not really bring the past any
nearer simply because they have existed, in one form or another,
over a period of ten, twenty or a hundred generations. Landscape alters continuously. Gibbon when he trod with lofty
step the ruins of the Forum was treading for the most part
twenty or thirty feet higher than the footsteps of antiquity,
though he did not use 'lofty' in that sense. Allowing for
erosion, preservation and repair, very few surfaces of ancient
things are in fact wholly ancient, and neither the ink nor the
paper of that distracted complaint of the indiscipline of the
Royalist cavalry, which I was reading last week, look the same
to me as they did to Colonel John Boys, the governor of
Donnington Castle, who wrote it, or to Prince Rupert who
received it, in the spring of 1644.

It is not always the place itself but some element in it which,
fused with our living knowledge, may suddenly vitalize the
past. Some years ago in Switzerland I came almost by accident
on the birthplace of Zwingli in the Toggenburg. The wooden
peasant's house had been a good deal smartened up and restored.
It had also been carefully furnished—in the praiseworthy and
instructive modern manner—with such objects as would give

the visitor an idea of a typical farmhouse interior at the latter end of the fifteenth century. But the house and all in it were vivid for me because I had lived for some months in childhood in a relatively modern farmhouse on the farther side of Switzerland, which was built on exactly the same plan. This is interesting evidence no doubt of the continuity of tradition in the building of Swiss farmhouses. But its immediate importance for me was that it brought a whole section of the past into my line of vision, almost into my personal experience: because I knew what it was like to live in such a house; knew the snug comfort of the wooden walls with the shutters closed at night, and the genial warmth from the oven, and—making considerable allowances for the differences between life in the last quarter of the fifteenth century and life in the first quarter of the twentieth—there remained at least a certain over-lapping experience between Ulrich Zwingli and me.

Marc Bloch has said in those valuable and fragmentary reflections on *The Historian's Craft*, which he wrote during his years in the Resistance, and which were published posthumously after his capture and death, that the historian can only, in the last analysis, reconstruct the past by borrowing from, and applying, his own daily experience of life. Jacob Burckhardt was expressing the same idea in a rather different form when he described the purpose of his lectures to his students in Basle: he wished, he said, ' to make every member of my audience feel and know that everyone may and must take independent possession of what appeals to him personally.' ' Take independent possession ' is the key phrase; for ultimately the understanding of the past, in so far as it is achieved at all, has to be independently achieved, by a sustained effort of the imagination working on a personal accumulation of knowledge and experience.

It was just this imaginative effort which the Romantics forced upon—or bequeathed to—historical scholarship. The foremost figure in this development was Sir Walter Scott. Leslie Stephen put the matter briefly and effectively when he spoke of the great step made by Scott when he observed that our ancestors were once ' as really alive as we are now.' The fashion for Sir Walter Scott's novels, not in the British Isles alone but over all western Europe, probably did more than any other single influence to awaken the minds of educated people to the vitality of the past. This is attested by the strongest possible witness, all the more telling because he is not altogether a favourable one. Leopold von Ranke has recorded, in an autobiographical fragment, the effect which the works of Scott had on him as a young man.

" The romantic historical works of Sir Walter Scott, which were well known in all languages and to all nations " (he writes), " played a principal part in awakening my sympathy for the actions and passions of past ages. On me too they exercised their spell and I read his works more than once with the most lively interest. But I was also offended by them. Among other things it distressed me that in *Quentin Durward* he treated Charles the Bold and Louis XI in a manner quite contrary to historical evidence . . . Comparison convinced me that historical statements are more beautiful and in any case more interesting than romantic fiction. I turned away altogether from the latter and resolved that in my own works I would neither invent nor poeticise anything but would confine myself strictly to the facts."

There are two parts of this confession of Ranke, and the last half—the criticism of *Quentin Durward*—is very often quoted without reference to what precedes it. First Ranke admits and indeed emphasizes that Scott had made history a living interest to thousands of readers, and had therefore brought into being for the historian a larger and a more sympathetic audience than ever before. Only then does he go on to express his distress at the shortcomings of *Quentin Durward* as a work of history, and so to dedicate himself to the establishment of fact pure and unadorned. In the introduction to his first major work he reiterated this dedication in the form in which it is best known, and declared that it is the historian's task only to show what actually happened (' Er will bloss zeigen wie es eigentlich gewesen '). The ideal was not one that could be realized, but if Sir Walter Scott can claim the credit not only for awakening a new public but also for starting Ranke on his career of fruitful and massive achievement, our debt to him becomes greater than ever. Those who are sensitive for the honour of Scott as a student of history may also reflect that if the young Ranke had confined his attention to *Old Mortality*, *Rob Roy*, *Heart of Midlothian* and those novels in which Scott is historically and geographically at home with his subject, he would not have found him playing half so many novelist's tricks with his material.

But though the scholar may protest at the inaccuracy of the novelist or the dramatist, the imaginative writer undoubtedly brings to history a more concentrated creative power than the pure scholar usually possesses, and for that reason, however much his actual presentation may leave to be desired, he can more easily capture the interest of the beginner. This is a psychological fact that scholars have from time to time recognized: Marc Bloch wryly admitted that ' readers of Alexandre Dumas may be potential historians '.

How far the novelist, the dramatist or the poet may take liberties with historical material is a question which has often

28

been debated, and it is a little surprising that Ranke, in his youthful innocence, expected Sir Walter Scott to treat the facts with scrupulous respect, for neither Schiller nor Goethe had done so in their dramas. Lessing had positively stated that the poet is master of history ('der Dichter ist Herr uber die Geschichte'), and had scolded Wieland for too slavishly following the facts in his play about Lady Jane Grey. Lady Jane's husband was weak, her father-in-law was ambitious and unpleasant; it would have made a better drama, Lessing argued, if Wieland had made proper use of his poetic licence to give greater nobility to these two characters.

A generation later Schiller, who as a professor and writer of history often showed a penetrating insight into the material available to him, stated the case for the use or abuse of historical material very interestingly in his criticism of Goethe's *Egmont*. The poet, he argued, can know, or not know—that is: he can use or disregard—the facts as best suits his treatment, but he ought not to leave out or misrepresent anything that is an integral part of the historical theme which he has selected. Goethe, in *Egmont*, has given his hero a sweet and loving mistress Clarchen; in order to do this he has eliminated Egmont's wife and nine (or perhaps eleven) children. Now Schiller argues that the tragedy of Egmont was the tragedy of a rooted and established man, tied by domestic, financial and family bonds to remain in the Netherlands and await the fatal coming of Alva, and that to take away his family is to alter the nature of his predicament, and consequently the nature of the conflict and calculations which delivered him into the hands of Alva when he might have sought safety—as the Prince of Orange did—in flight. Goethe's tragedy is consequently a very beautiful and touching tragedy about a simple, noble and trusting man, but it is not about the historic Egmont at all. This is sound and well argued, and is all the more impressive because in his *History of the Revolt of the Netherlands* Schiller's portait of Egmont is a full and careful piece of historical characterization. What Schiller said in his criticism of Goethe is very much what Ranke was later to say of Scott—that the simple historical facts are more interesting and more revealing of human problems than any inventions can be. Yet when Schiller came to write his play on Joan of Arc, none of these wise considerations prevented him from making her die in the hour of victory on the battle-field, tenderly supported on either hand by Charles VII and the Duke of Burgundy—a disregard of facts that destroys the true poignant climax of Saint Joan's life; compared with such tampering Goethe's liquidation of the entire Egmont family is trivial.

Much can be said against the romantic approach to history. It tended too easily to the theatrical and the fanciful; also it came into being at an epoch when the conviction that human life was a constant, forward progress towards an attainable perfection was very strong. The romantic attitude to the past was therefore heavily tainted with the belief that the past existed chiefly to lead up to, and make way for, the glorious present and still more glorious future. Tennyson's hero of ' Locksley Hall '—' heir of all the ages in the foremost files of time '—is only echoing Schiller's inaugural lecture at Jena: ' Ours are all the treasures which industry and genius, reason and experience have gathered in during the long ages of the world.' This inspiring frame of mind easily degenerated into the smugness which treated the past chiefly as something which could be compared to its disadvantage with the present, so as to demonstrate gratifying human progress. This was a commonplace of the nineteenth and even of the early twentieth century. *We* no longer believe in witchcraft. *We* no longer burn people alive for their religious beliefs. *We* have abolished public executions and installed bathrooms almost everywhere. How much more tolerant, how much cleaner, how much better we are than our forebears!

From this it is an easy step to regarding as worthy of study only such institutions and only such persons as can be shown to have some clear connection with the present, and of seeing or imagining in them only such elements as can be made to fit into the splendid story of progress towards the political or social ideal as we happen to see it. The tribal chieftain fighting the Romans, or the feudal baron defying his overlord became the conscious vindicators of nationalism or of representative government. More recently the leaders of peasant revolts have come to be hailed as the apostles of popular rights and modern democracy. The dialogue in Shaw's *Saint Joan* where the Earl of Warwick and the Bishop of Beauvais discuss the disturbing emergence of forces which they diagnose as liberalism and nationalism can be taken as an apt and ironical comment on the remarkably modern ideas and moods which even some writers of great learning have managed to detect in the past. From these misapprehensions the descent is quick towards the deliberate use of history to sustain whatever view of politics or morality suits the propagandist or the party in power.

In spite of all these drawbacks, possibly even because of them, the romantic approach to history made the understanding of the past possible in ways never attempted before. The romantics recognized the comprehensive nature of history as a study. ' In dem Gebiet der Geschichte liegt die ganze moralische Welt,' said Schiller in the same inaugural lecture at Jena, for him, the entire moral world was contained in history. There was no province of human endeavour outside the scope of history. To this general conception the romantics added the conviction that history can only be studied by entering sympathetically into the thought and feeling of the past.

This is an entirely subjective approach. The moment the student of history came into the inheritance of the romantic writers and took cognisance of the fact that his ancestors had been as much alive as he was himself, he could use his own living experience to imagine and project himself into their state of being. Nothing else would serve. The dangers of this technique are apparent, but so also are its merits. The alternative, the pre-romantic view, the approach of which Edward Gibbon is the most accomplished exponent, has its own brilliant clarity but the historian remains always at a distance from the events described, and gives the impression sometimes almost of inhumanity. To Gibbon, history really is ' little more than the register of the crimes, follies, and misfortunes of mankind '. ' Register ' is a significant word. He can describe very vividly, but he constantly utters asides, or halts by the way for general reflection and comment, and by so doing he keeps the historic moment, and the men involved in it, at a safe distance both from himself and from the reader. The thunder-bolts are being hurled far below the eminence on which Gibbon sits. Look for instance at his account of the murder of the Emperor Pertinax by the Praetorian Guard and the subsequent auction of the imperial title in the year A.D. 193. Gibbon describes the event with considerable drama—the ' two or three hundred of the most desperate soldiers ' marching at noon through Rome ' with arms in their hands and fury in their looks, towards the Imperial Palace ', then their confrontation by the grave and undaunted Emperor and his death. At this Gibbon concludes the chapter; he begins the next with an account of the origin and character of the Praetorian Guard—' Such formidable servants are always necessary, but often fatal, to the throne of despotism '—and after this interlude which has broken the tension and removed us to a comfortable distance, he returns to the appalling scene from which he withdrew at the end of the previous chapter:

" Amidst the wild disorder Sulpicianus the emperor's father-in-law, and governor of the city, who had been sent to the camp on the first alarm of mutiny, was endeavouring to calm the fury of the multitude, when he was silenced by the clamorous return of the murderer, bearing on a lance the head of Pertinax. Though history has accustomed us to observe every principle and every passion yielding to the imperious dictates of ambition, it is scarcely credible that, in these moments of horror, Sulpicianus should have aspired to ascend a throne polluted with the recent blood of so near a relation, and so excellent a prince. He had already begun to use the only effectual argument, and to treat for the imperial dignity; but the more prudent of the Praetorians, apprehensive that in this private contract they should not obtain a just price for so valuable a commodity, ran out upon the ramparts and, with a loud voice, proclaimed that the Roman world was to be disposed of to the best bidder by public auction."

Again Gibbon breaks into the middle of the shocking event with a general reflection on the power of ambition over the human mind; and possibly because he removes himself, with a not unnatural distaste, from the predicament of Sulpicianus surrounded by the mutinous Praetorian Guard bent on slaughter, it does not occur to him that in this particular case Sulpicianus is more likely to have been actuated by downright fear than by ambition. Surely Gibbon, had he been surrounded by this gang of murderers, would have admitted that fear was a powerful motive for anything that he then did. In what way, except by offering them money and at the same time trying to establish some authority over them, was the unfortunate Sulpicianus to get out of a very awkward place? Gibbon cannot and does not imagine himself in the predicament of Sulpicianus and an obvious element in the situation therefore escapes him. Gibbon's method enables him to describe and explore the surface of events with incomparable brilliance, but it rarely leads to any penetration below the surface. He does not, for instance, ask the question which must immediately occur to any modern reader of his account of the reign and fall of Pertinax—how came it that Pertinax who, according to Gibbon was both able, virtuous and beloved of the people, played his cards so badly that he came to grief after a reign of only eighty-six days?

In the post-romantic age such brilliant mapping of the surface of human events gives place to bold and by no means always successful attempts to penetrate the inner meaning, and human motives behind them. I have just made such an attempt myself, for I know nothing whatever about the character of Sulpicianus and may be wrong in suggesting that he would have been actuated on this occasion by the fear which would certainly have actuated me in his position—and which I believe would have actuated Edward Gibbon—but in the absence of more particular and definite evidence it seems a reasonable assumption that he was thinking at least a little of the immediate danger in which he stood.

Leaving aside the question of the interpretation of character (the most complicated, interesting and insoluble problem), the insistence of the romantics on the reality of past happenings, their strenuous demand that events should be thought out with the fullest sympathy, led as a natural result to a continual enlarging of historic inquiry. For though some confused imagination with fantasy and were content to imagine *in vacuo*, weaving ideas and images about the past from no knowledge at all, those

34

seriously interested in the past fixed their imaginative ideas on anything and everything that they could find out about it. Hence, first the more or less sentimental attachment to places and things. Hence—it is triumphantly present in Scott—the desire to know about the physical surroundings, the leisure occupations, the way of living in all ranks of society, the food and drink, the ways of thought of our ancestors; and so ultimately to the widening of historical inquiry, beyond the political, the legal and the military, to embrace the social, the economic and all those branches of research and learning which are an integral part of historical study today.

But the act of imagination was often made with a glib and deceptive facility. The inquirer tended to over-emphasize all characteristics of thought and feeling that resembled his own, and even to see resemblances that were not there. Only gradually did students come to recognize the necessity for continual adjustments, for eliminating from our perspective of the past certain ways of thought which seem natural and essential to us but which did not always seem so.

Historians bred in the idea of national loyalty as almost a natural law found it extremely difficult to grasp the meaning of the different loyalties, no less strong, which have controlled and disciplined the political lives of men in the past. The meaning and sanctity of oaths is subject to infinite variations, and very few words like ' treason ', ' fidelity ', ' betrayal ', mean exactly the same in contexts separated by long stretches of time. Meanwhile school text-books still to a great extent impose the idea that national history is the primary sort of history and thus create an unnatural division of the subject.

Our whole attitude to history, the framework within which we think of the past, the premises from which we explore and rediscover it, spring from habits of thought which are not themselves permanent. Thus, we think of ourselves as occupying a specific place in time; and of the individual life as interwoven with a continuous fabric of lives on this planet, past and future, stretching back and stretching forward. For us Man stands— or we ourselves stand—*historically* between Past and Future. This habit of thought which developed gradually in the Renaissance and Reformation has now become unconscious and instinctive with us. Whatever depth of religious faith we may also possess, we habitually think and calculate in these material terms, in a sequence of cause and effect over the years; we make deductions from the past and apply them to the future, in our own lives and in contemporary politics. In fact we think *historically*, and a very considerable effort is necessary if we are to adjust our way of thinking to a quite different outlook.

We only have to go a few centuries back in the history of Europe, to the Middle Ages, to find men framing their thought and action on entirely different assumptions. For them the individual life was set not in time, but in eternity; ideas and actions were to be thought of not in terms of time past and time future, but in terms of eternity in Heaven or Hell. This attitude persisted for many years alongside the way of thought which we have adopted and, in the sixteenth and seventeenth century either, and both, were possible. This different outlook makes religious persecution seem, if not less deplorable, at least more comprehensible.

The historian who fails to make allowance for these deep changes in ways of human thought is unlikely to develop an illuminating sense of the past. Without the capacity for entering into the fervour of our ancestors' beliefs we shall never gain any real understanding of the Reformation. Ranke said that to write justly of that earthquake epoch the historian must forget that he is a Catholic or a Protestant, but his advice is not altogether wise because a better account of the Reformation is more likely to come from the writer who is fanatical in some belief, than from one incapable of any. Our forefathers have been more traduced by those who interpret the Reformation purely as an economic, or purely as a political, conflict than by the violent partisans of either side.

A more subtle and continuous obstacle to the development of a sense of the past is that, simply by his position in time, the modern student knows too much. When he contemplates a past situation he is aware in some measure of what succeeded it and of how it was resolved. When he examines the motives and actions of an individual he knows already what their results will be. None of this knowledge formed a part of the situation at the time. Yet it is nearly impossible to expel it from the mind and to study a problem of the past as though the outcome was still unknown. I long in vain for the innocence I had when, as a child, I went to see John Drinkwater's play *Abraham Lincoln* without any previous instruction. (Its historical accuracy is not here relevant; what changes he made were mostly in the interests of dramatic simplification.) Since I knew that right ought to triumph, I guessed at an early stage that this admirable ugly man in the funny top hat would be certain to win the war and liberate the slaves, but nothing had prepared me for the appearance and behaviour of John Wilkes Booth, and for me at least the dummy pistol shot in a London theatre in the nineteen-twenties came as a shock almost as horrifying as that experienced by spectators at Ford's Theatre in Washington on 15 April 1865.

In vain have I longed to recapture that blessed ignorance— to be able for instance to consider the policy of William the Silent in the difficult year after he withdrew from Antwerp in July 1583, without the nagging knowledge that Balthasar Gerard is steadily drawing nearer, and that on 10 July 1584 he will put an end to the Prince of Orange's life and throw all his policies out of gear. In its perfect state—if such could be reached —the sense of the past should carry with it a capacity for eliminating the consciousness of the future, so that we could examine and consider the quality of an epoch *for itself alone*, without any attention to what came after it.

There is here an antagonism between two ways of looking at history, both interesting, both legitimate, but devoted to quite different ends. It is a valuable study, for instance, to trace the growth of the party system in English Parliamentary government. We can distinguish and map its origins in the earlier half of the seventeenth century and note the increasing tension between crown officials, courtiers and court nominees on the one hand, and those who were outside the Court Circle. In the present state of our knowledge the growth of two parties, Court and Country, Tory and Whig, can be more or less clearly traced and demonstrated. But such a demonstration is relevant to the present rather than to the past. It is interesting because of what has happened *since* in English Parliamentary life, but too much emphasis on it inevitably colours, and falsely colours, our attitude to what was actually happening in Parliament at the time, what men thought was happening, and what elements in the situation they themselves recognized and valued.

In the autumn of 1641, when the war between King Charles I and Parliament was rapidly approaching, and the House of Commons was very bitterly divided between the supporters of John Pym and his opponents, Dr. William Chillingworth was sent to the Tower for having incautiously referred, in a private conversation, to the existence of two sides in the House of Commons. This was denounced as a highly dangerous and subversive statement because the House of Commons was, they most strenuously believed, a single and united body; one contemporary writer did not scruple to compare it to 'the seamless robe of Christ.' Of course, every sensible Parliament man in the autumn of 1641 could see quite plainly that there *were* two sides in the House; but not one of them had the additional advantage of knowing that this was the beginning of the famous two party system, a useful political invention of which their descendants would justly boast. On the contrary they thought it disastrous; they saw it as contrary to all that they believed about the function of Parliament, and they pretended that it had not happened. Pym's followers explained the fatal split in the House by assuming that *they* were the true House of Commons and the only party of the Commonweal, and that the King's supporters were a 'malignant faction.' The King's supporters, with equal sincerity, assumed that they were the true and undivided House of Commons and the others a 'juggling junto', deliberately sowing division in the councils of the nation and manœuvring for personal power.

It is easier to understand the ultimate development of Parliamentary government in England by tracing the party system to its origins; but we shall understand the Civil War and the Long Parliament better if we realize, not merely objectively, as a quaint oddity, but with full intellectual sympathy, how repugnant this idea of a divided Parliament was to the men of the time.

In a somewhat different sense from that which Schiller had in mind when he said that the poet was at liberty to know or not to know historical facts as it suited him, the historian, who really wants to understand a situation as it was, must also know, and not know; he must accumulate one kind of knowledge, everything immediate to a particular situation, and reject another kind—everything which subsequently sprang from that situation, or came after it. He must divest his mind as far as he can—and it will not be very far—of the wisdom, the philosophy, the prejudices, the ways of thought and social behaviour that belong to his own age; in their place he must try to learn and—temporarily at least—to make his mind accept, the ideas of a quite different epoch. It goes without saying that this cannot be done without a formidable accumulation of evidence for the mind to work on.

The romantic attitude to history—this projection of sympathy into a past age—led to certain follies and excesses, and to a sentimental facility in summoning up ready-made emotions about places and things associated with the past. It led on the one hand to a picturesque idealization and poeticization of history, but it also led to a much more human and vivid appreciation of the past fate and actions of men. It encouraged in the serious inquirer a more accurate and a much fuller conception of the past. It led him to make a sustained effort fully to understand, or in Burckhardt's phrase 'to possess' the past. He tried—and still tries—to take hold of it through knowledge, and through imagination working on knowledge, so that the sense of the past is in the end no vague and hollow dream, but something based on wide and minute comprehension of assembled facts.

In the illuminating notes which Henry James left on that projected and unfinished novel, *The Sense of the Past*, he describes the increasingly painful predicament in which his hero was to have found himself during his intrusion into a previous century. It was one thing, Henry James wrote, 'to live in the Past with the whole spirit, the whole candour of confidence and confidence of candour, that he would then naturally have had—and a totally different thing to find himself living in it without those helps to possibility, those determinations of relation, those preponderant right instincts and saving divinations'.

Poor lost young man! But the historian need not (even in

the gardens of Versailles) either fear or hope for one of those kinks or knots in time, dear to writers, that will project him suddenly into an earlier epoch. He will remain fixed and rooted in his own time with nothing but evidence, imagination and his own experience to minister to the ' sense of the past '. He may have now and again, an occasional flash of those ' right instincts and saving divinations ', but he can never hope to acquire, however long and laborious the study, that ' confidence of candour and candour of confidence ' that our ancestors had in their own age; and that we have only in ours.

# PRINCIPLES AND PERSPECTIVES

EVERY SCHOLAR and every writer who seriously embarks on the study of history must sooner or later become aware of the moral problems which that study involves and must take measures to solve them. Whether the historian embarks upon some all-embracing account of world events and seeks to find a pattern and meaning for the whole story of man, or whether he confines himself to a brief period and a small region, say the administrative history of Galloway during the minority of King David II, he will be dealing with the actions of men, though seen in a different perspective and on a different scale. He may lean by temperament towards the romantic and biographical approach so that history is for him dominated by the deeds and ideas of great men and women and foot-noted with anecdotes of their lives; or he may pursue his studies in impersonal terms, seeing men and women as merely incidental to the evolution of institutions, to the rise and fall of societies, the interplay of economic forces; he may devote himself to the personal career of Napoleon, or the decay of the feudal system, or spend a lifetime compiling from the available sources, figures showing the number of vessels trading to Hamburg during the Thirty Years War and the character of their cargoes. But he must always at some point become aware of the desire to say that such a thing was good or bad, such an action right or wrong. He may believe this to be an important part of the historian's function and have no doubts in his mind as to how it should be done. He may hold that moral judgments are no part of his task and dismiss from his mind all conscious thought of them. But however strongly he may believe in the dispassionate approach, if he is honest with himself he will know that his opinions and his judgments are the outcome of the personal beliefs, fears and prejudices implanted in his mind by the people with whom he grew up and the events in the world about him, and that these things will show in his work, if not openly, then between the lines.

It is impossible for the historian to avoid making value judgments and it is difficult for him to define precisely on what grounds he makes them. Quite apart from the numerous moral and political prejudices to which he is subject, the dimension of time adds a further complication. Great distances of time reduce the intensity with which we feel about moral issues. What Cromwell did to the people of Wexford is much closer in time, and therefore much more imaginable, and therefore much more distressing, than what the Emperor Theodosius did to the people of Thessalonica. Questions of right and wrong, of humanity and inhumanity ought to be equally significant to the historian whatever the period in which they happen. But it is evident that they are not; few accounts of the September massacres are written without some sign of passion or sympathy on one side or the other, but the story of the Sicilian Vespers can be told with apparent detachment.

The history of a nation as told by a foreigner, and as told by a native are totally different things; the same history may look different again if told by a member of a dominant group or of a minority. It is not only that the appearance of facts changes, that the Union of 1707 does not look the same to an Englishman and to a Scot, or that the American Civil War reveals

43

wholly different aspects to a native of New England and to a native of South Carolina. The perspective and the emphasis, the relationship between different facts and their relative importance also changes. In the changing perspectives of time and place the intelligence and the morality of almost all actions, the virtues and the vices, the advantages and disadvantages of almost all events, can be, and are, differently assessed. The right of one generation is the wrong of another, the right of one nation or class is the wrong of another.

Liberal historians of the nineteenth century believed in progress and believed that the creation of nation states and the liberation of oppressed peoples were a right and proper part of progress. Most of them also believed that toleration, variously equated with Rationalism or Protestantism, was also right, though this clear and simple alignment occasionally caused embarrassment. What for instance was Samuel Rawson Gardiner to do with the Irish Rebellion of 1641? He could not deny that this rising was a fervent expression of national spirit and he accorded a cautious approval to this noble feeling. But no one had explained to the Irish that, to satisfy liberal historians of a later date that they were properly equipped for setting up a nation state, they should have been Protestants—like for instance the Dutch whose revolt against Philip II was much and rightly applauded by liberal-minded historians.

The Irish were emphatically not Protestants, and more in sorrow than in anger, Gardiner had to point out that their rising was thus doomed from the outset not because they were, after ten years, outnumbered and out-gunned by the Puritan English, but because they were "throwing themselves athwart the line of historical progress." This would be more convincing as an explanation of failure if all Catholic-national revolts at this epoch could be shown to have collapsed. But Gardiner had overlooked, strangely, the exactly contemporaneous revolt of Portugal against Spain. The Portuguese, of whose national fervour there is no question, also made the same mistake as the Irish; they were nationalist without being Protestant. But they threw themselves athwart the line of historical progress with complete success.

Generalizations, even from the most learned and judicious writers, often come to look foolish when the beliefs which made them acceptable have lost their force. That might be a warning against making generalizations at all, but the historian cannot do entirely without a moral and political framework within which to arrange his facts and make his deductions. The past has to be measured as the present is measured against the standards and beliefs on which, consciously or unconsciously, the historian conducts his own life.

This is the first paradox. The things which we believe to be right, the things which we believe to be true, vary widely from age to age and the same holds good for the past times which are the historian's province. If we make no allowance for these variations we become rigid and stultified, lacking in human imagination, unable to bring full understanding either to the present or to the past, accepting received ideas and traditional prejudices instead of judging for ourselves. If we make too much allowance for the changing of standards and the shifting of opinions we begin to lose all sense of moral stability. Historical thinking has always fluctuated between these two dangers, the danger of having no perspective at all, and the danger of having one only; the danger of having no principles at all and the danger of having principles that are too rigid.

It has recently been most persuasively argued by the scientist philosopher Professor Michael Polanyi in *The Study of Man* that historians by emphasizing the relativity of moral standards and their inconstant shiftings from age to age have exercised an important influence in undermining, or at least unsteadying, our capacities to make moral judgments. The accusation deserves serious consideration. The original intention of historians, when they argued that men should be judged strictly within the framework of their own time, was a generous one. It arose from the desire to do justice to men and motives in the past. This was also a sound idea, in relation to enquiry, because it is evident that the historian who has a full understanding of the principles and standards of the people and societies he is studying will be able to interpret the evidence they have left behind them with a far better prospect of discovering the truth than the historian who is without this understanding or has it only in a very imperfect degree.

The wars of religion have left their mark on the institutions, the society and the prejudices of most of the peoples of western Europe. These bitter and distracting conflicts are not only dismal and deplorable but largely incomprehensible until we can bring to them some understanding of the beliefs which guided the protagonists. We must understand and accept the idea that, however self-interested their conduct may appear, the rulers of that epoch (all of them in theory and many of them in practice) believed that it was their duty and their function to legislate for their people not only in time but in eternity: that they were responsible in the first place for their subjects' souls and only in the second place (if at all) for their physical welfare on earth.

The examination of the economic revolution caused by these religious troubles and of the economic motives which were undeniably important throws much light on certain aspects of the subject, but it does not illumine the whole. It must be added to, and not substituted for, an understanding of the spiritual issues involved. It is, incidentally, a curious symptom of our own time that the purely materialist interpretation of history, and the present popularity of economic determinism are at least in part a moral and spiritual revolt against the uncertainty and fluidity of historicism. The aggressively materialist view of the historical process was seized upon by many, from my own generation onwards, to satisfy a spiritual thirst, the thirst for certainty, which the historicists left unsatisfied.

Historicism, this way of thinking about the past, or attempting to think about it in its own terms, was the outcome of an idea both humane and scholarly. But it had and still has very grave dangers as Lord Acton clearly saw and as clearly taught. He never ceased to exhort postulant historians to apply, in the last resort, the highest ethical standards to their historical judgments. " In judging men and things," he wrote to Creighton, " ethics go before dogma, politics and nationality." Belief in the moral law must lie at the root of all sound historical judgment. Failing this, the historian, in trying to apply different standards to different epochs, will confuse himself, and ultimately his readers, by taking the explanation of conduct for the justification of it. We cannot understand why King Philip II imposed the Council of Blood on his subjects in the Netherlands, or why Cromwell massacred the Irish unless we understand the beliefs which made them hold these things to be right and just. But explanation is not justification: these things were not in themselves right and just. Given the framework of belief within which King Philip II or Oliver Cromwell reasoned, we can say that their own responsibility for actions in themselves evil was relatively less than was, for instance, the responsibility of Hitler for actions in themselves evil. The religious beliefs and the moral standards of the sixteenth and seventeenth centuries on the whole supported these atrocious actions. That does not make evil actions in themselves less evil, but it makes the motives

47

of those who perform them less depraved. It was possible in the sixteenth and seventeenth centuries for very evil things to be done by men who were not necessarily evil, who were even, on balance, good men. The same argument could hardly be sustained, at least as far as racial and religious persecution is concerned, in the twentieth century. But to say that those who perform evil actions are less culpable at some times and in some contexts than they are in others, is not to minimize the evil of the actions themselves. The confusion is all too easily made; from explaining an action we move insensibly towards justifying it, and from thence towards a general blurring of the moral issues and a comfortable belief that circumstances are always to blame, and men and women are not.

This is the confusion into which historians fall when they make allowances for " the standards of the age ". Their intention is to understand and be just to the past, but the result in the long run may be unfair to the present, because this outlook steadily and stealthily fosters the conviction that nothing is good or bad in itself but only in relation to its surroundings.

Historians who subscribe to this view fall into two classes according to temperament. If by temperament they are mainly interested in people, that is in individual human problems, they will act in the belief that to understand all is to forgive all. *Tout comprendre c'est tout pardonner*: discover all the relevant facts, make the imaginative effort to understand why a particular man took a particular decision or performed a particular act, and it will be possible to view his conduct, however deplorable or however vicious, with a dispassionate benevolence.

This is neither wise, sensible nor responsible conduct. The aspiration to understand and to forgive is noble and valid in personal relationships between the living. It is also, in actual and everyday personal relationships, by no means easy to achieve.

It is harder to understand and to forgive the personal irritations and annoyances, let alone the wrongs, that we suffer or think we suffer at the hands of our contemporaries than it is to forgive all the crimes of the Emperor Domitian. The first requires an effort in self-control and self-forgetfulness, and some sacrifice of personal pride; the second is merely an intellectual exercise. The application of the principle of understanding and forgiveness to historical personages is a sentimental fallacy. The historian has suffered nothing at their hands; it is not for him to pronounce an absolution. But it is for him to make sure that the crime or crimes really were as they have been handed down, and that their authors were the people to whom they have been attributed. That is the proper function of the historian, but that is quite a different story.

If the historian deals rather with impersonal matters, with the development of institutions, with mass-movements, with the growth and decline of societies or ideas, this "historicist" attitude may cause him simply to suspend conscious judgment: to discover, to record, but to make no open comment. A concealed and perhaps unintentional comment he will be hardly able to avoid. He may trace the origins of the Inquisition, explain its function and its practices, consider what made it appear necessary and be endurable to the society which created and sustained it; but he will desist from openly saying whether it was good or bad. It simply *was* and is to be considered dispassionately in relation to its historical background. He may study the institution of slavery through the ages, noting its various forms from the ancient world to the present time. He may examine the effects of the system on the societies which practised it, and the different conditions under which slaves have lived at different times and in different parts of the world, but if he holds to the view that no judgment should be made except in relation to the standards of the epoch, he will offer no explicit opinion on the institution itself. The people who accepted the system evidently approved of it, and once the idea is accepted that an epoch or a society should only be judged on its own terms, there is nothing further for the historian to say.

This sentimentality in judging people, and this refusal to judge things, both arise from the highest of motives, the desire to be just. Historicism has undoubtedly deepened and widened the outlook of historians and of their readers. The historians who wrote before the idea of historicism had been developed have greater assurance in their own wisdom; their words have an air of confident moral and political authority; but they can be strangely narrow. It did not occur to Voltaire or to Gibbon to look at the actions of their forefathers from any angle but their own. In our own era of confused issues and tottering principles, the great eighteenth century historians are a tonic to read because of their unhesitating certainty and their conviction of their own well-grounded reasonableness. But their vision as historians, though detailed and clear, was limited. They could make no sense of points of view widely different from their own or institutions that they did not understand. What they did not understand they scorned. Few of them could penetrate, for instance, the Gothic gloom which, for them, obscured the lively society of Europe's middle ages.

This was left to the romantics, when the Age of Reason had been shocked into its grave by the French Revolution. The romantics, above all, influenced historians towards the adoption of a more sympathetic attitude towards individuals, and a more tentative, more eager and inquiring, less contemptuous approach to extraordinary ideas and unfamiliar institutions. Of all the romantics Sir Walter Scott had the widest influence on the

approach to history not only in Great Britain but over the
whole of Western Europe, for he wanted, like all writers of
imagination, to be on terms with his characters, whether they
were intended for contemporary figures, or drawn from the
past. This was equally true whether he was writing novels or
history, whether he was drawing an imaginary figure or one
like Rob Roy or Montrose for whom he had genuine material
to use. This desire to be on good terms with his characters made
him take pains to find out how they would have thought and
felt. He was not always successful in this, but the effort and the
intention were always there. He wanted to talk the language of
the past with the men of the past. The pre-romantic historians
had no such desires. If by some midsummer magic in the Eildon
Hills, where True Thomas met the Færy Queen, Walter Scott
had found a means of conversing with men and women of
bygone centuries, he would have embraced it with joy. But
would Edward Gibbon have done so? In the first place he
would not have believed the thing possible. But even if it had
been possible, he hardly wished for any closer acquaintance with
Belisarius or the Emperor Julian than he had already acquired;
let the centuries keep their distance.

The study of modern history as we know it, in all its depth
and richness, owes much to the romantics and to historicism.
But as understanding increased and sympathies became more
fluid moral certainties declined. Scott himself was a child of the
eighteenth century, and the assured standards of the Age of
Reason prevented his generation from carrying the principles,
or rather the lack of principle, of historicism to its logical con-
clusion. In ensuing generations, as historical scholarship became
ever more extensive and more detailed, the danger increased.
The youthful Ranke greatly intensified it by setting up the ideal
of dispassionate truth. All preconceived views, all religious and

political prejudices must be set aside: the historian's task was to find out and state " what actually happened." This was a noble ideal but it was also impossible of achievement, and rigidly applied it certainly implied the abdication of any function of moral judgment.

Ranke did not—indeed he could not—live up to his ideal. His pupil Burckhardt, the least deceived of nineteenth century historians, viewed the great illusion of the master with a kind of exasperated admiration. While he stood amazed and in awe before the gigantic learning and the colossal achievement of Ranke—the volume upon volume of European history, much of it based on pioneer research—he was amused and irritated by the way in which the great man slid his personal prejudices into his writing under his superficially dispassionate manner, and constantly implied value judgments often of an extremely simple kind. He admired the clarity and vitality of his mind and his indefatigable energy, but he was irritated and sometimes shocked by his naïveté, his self-deception and at times his small mindedness. It is not irrelevant to record that in 1870 Ranke, the apostle of the dispassionate approach to history, could justify the Franco-Prussian war on the grounds that " we are fighting against Louis XIV "; a classic example of misapplied history and deep national prejudice.

The sincerity and the genuine idealism of Ranke's conception of dispassionate history won for it a wide acceptance. But though nothing could sound more noble than the dispassionate pursuit of truth, the ultimate effect of this teaching was to be sadly ignoble. History dispassionately recorded nearly always sounds harsh and cynical. History is not a moral tale, and the effect of telling it without comment is, inevitably, to underline its worst features: the defeat of the weak by the strong, the degeneration of ideals, the corruption of institutions, the triumph of intelligent self-interest. It was no accident that the age of Ranke was also the age of Realpolitik.

A subsequent and yet more disturbing development was to follow from this elevation of the idea of dispassionate truth. On almost every historical point, except the simplest, it is very hard to establish truth. Napoleon once rudely described history as " une fable convenue "; but an agreed fable, a generally accepted legend, can provide a stable and comfortable background. When the new disciplines and techniques of historical research were turned upon the various agreed fables which had served men well enough for several generations, these fables naturally disintegrated. They were replaced not by new, better and more truthful fables, but by furious arguments. Over almost the whole field of history—especially modern history—the increase in knowledge has brought a decrease of certainty: too many perspectives and too few principles. The accepted designs were shattered, the recognisable forms and figures would no longer do, and history, like other forms of art, entered on a period of abstraction.

The violent times through which we have lived were not foreseen by Ranke, who believed confidently in progress. They were foreseen with uncanny accuracy by the more gloomy and more perceptive Burckhardt. Their effect on historical thinking has been, inevitably, to bring about a return to a more rigid and less fluid way of thought. On the one hand there is the revival of the almost religious attitude to history, the desire to find in it the handwriting of God and to deduce from our now enormously increased factual knowledge some idea of the pattern of world events past, present and to come. Hence the inspiration and the wide popularity of Toynbee's *Survey of History*: hence also the strong academic resistance to it. Hence the growth of the influence of determinist views of history.

History, told within the Marxist pattern, gives answers to all the important questions; they may not be the right answers, but to many people a definite answer is a right answer. For what they want from history is not the truth about the past—which only interests a very small minority—but ideas and directives for conduct in the present.

If such a demand exists, it is evidently more dangerous to leave it unsatisfied than to satisfy it. The great historians have rarely lost sight of their ultimate responsibility to their readers. Historicism enlarged and enriched the scholar's understanding of the past, but it left the present out of account. Dispassionate scholars to-day are vainly trying to hold a position, which they have themselves disintegrated and undermined, against the advance of the new and revived philosophies of history, which offer not a flickering and uncertain truth about the past, but plausible answers to insistent modern questions. The position can only be restored and held, as Acton saw, by the insistence on a moral standard.

# NICCOLO MACHIAVELLI

WHEN Niccolo Machiavelli, suitably attired in his coun-cillor's robes, withdrew from the living room of his poverty-stricken home to the refuge of his study to compose his two great political works, it was not his intention to start an argument that would last from the sixteenth century to the twentieth. On the contrary, he intended to formulate rules of statecraft which would put an end to argument. It occurred to him, as it has done to some greater and to many lesser men, that the lamentable confusion of contemporary society could be reduced to order if practical rules for political conduct could be established. He sought for those rules where men of learning in his age were accustomed to seek: in the superior wisdom of classical times. His *Discourses* are a penetrating analysis of the events recorded in the first ten books of Livy, and *The Prince*, although in a less explicit manner, derives equally from classical reading.

Machiavelli's material was typical Renaissance material; his way of looking at it was his own. He claimed to have entered upon a path " as yet untrodden by anyone else," and certainly his analysis of past history and of contemporary events and the conclusions he reached on correct political conduct in a great variety of circumstances impressed and astonished many of his contemporaries. Such a connoisseur of statecraft as Thomas Cromwell warmly recommended his works. Machiavelli's cardinal weakness, as Professor Butterfield has pointed out, is that his conviction of Roman superiority prevents him from approaching his material objectively. In spite of the preconception which partly governs his conclusions, Machiavelli remains a pioneer of the inductive method of reasoning, and by more than half a century the forerunner of Francis Bacon. Whether he is altogether to be praised for this innovation is more doubtful. A method which was to prove valuable in other spheres has particular dangers when applied to history. The material is too doubtful and imprecise to be suited to this treatment, a truth which escaped Machiavelli's penetrating intellect because of the relative simplicity of the historical evidence available to him. He was not particularly worried by conflicting or alternative versions of the facts which he analysed, still less by the existence of indefinable or imponderable elements in any given political situation, elements whose existence would, and indeed often does, make nonsense of his maxims. Nemesis overtook him, or rather his writings; for these very imponderables, these elements on which he had not reckoned, made his practical political handbooks objects of bitter opprobrium within a few years of his death.

He gained the notoriety which has more or less clung to his name ever since, because the nature of politics underwent a violent change in the middle years of the sixteenth century. It has sometimes been said that the divorce of politics from ethics begins with Machiavelli. This was not true in practice; politics and ethics have been through a series of marriages and divorces since the beginning of recorded history. Machiavelli happened to live at a time and in a country where this divorce appeared to be absolute; his observations rested on this assumption. Very shortly after his death European politics entered upon one of the most intensely religious phases through which they have ever passed. A violent reaction from Machiavelli's works was the direct consequence. He had calculated, with resignation, on the natural depravity of man, but he had also calculated that man would act on the whole as a reasonable being. *The Prince* places before rulers patterns of the coolest reason and common sense. The *Discourses* call for the exercise of these qualities by republican governments. The Reformation and the Counter-Reformation produced among a great number of people, and even among ruling princes, a frame of mind which was wholly unreasonable. Religious beliefs and moral convictions became dominating forces throughout western Europe. Individual princes or whole societies were found ready to run impossible risks and to make preposterous sacrifices in order to preserve or restore certain religious observances. Whatever ulterior motives the present fashion may attribute to the men of the Religious Wars there can be no serious doubt that many of them were moved by the most passionate sincerity. This supercharge of inspired irrationality gives to the events of the period an explosive and incalculable quality which cannot be explained merely in terms of social unrest and economic change.

The men of the Counter-Reformation repudiated Machiavelli with the frenetic zeal that they applied to most of their beliefs and prejudices, for he had denied by implication that element in politics which was to them of paramount importance, the salvation of the human soul. The unredeemed materialism of his outlook, though it might still appeal to a rare thinker like Francis Bacon or, with significant reservations, to a practical politician like Cardinal Richelieu, was repellent to the majority of men during the whole of that tumultuous religious century. The men of the new dispensation, particularly in the Roman Catholic Church, led the attack; Cardinal Pole declared that the author of *The Prince* was an " enemy of the human race."

Pope Paul IV put his works on the Index and the Council of Trent confirmed the condemnation. By one of those paradoxical twists very frequent in that age of fanaticism and propaganda, the Protestants attributed the practice of Machiavelli's doctrines —or what they believed to be his doctrines—to the Catholics in general and the Jesuits in particular. The identical compliment was returned with equal heat. Yet in the case of the Jesuits the slander struck so deep a root that even today Father Walker, Machiavelli's latest translator and editor in English, thinks it advisable in the introduction to his scholarly work specifically to repudiate Machiavelli's more obnoxious views.

Those who accepted the name of Machiavelli as a symbol for close designs and crooked counsels had not always read him. His ideas were so widely and slanderously disseminated at second and third hand that those who most religiously repudiated him often did so in ignorance of what he had actually taught. Only when the vehement rage of the Religious Wars had died down was it possible to look at his work again with a dispassionate eye and to discover with surprise that some of his doctrines were respectable and that all were presented with a precision and judgment which make his works an education to study. The unrelenting materialism is certainly there, but so are reflections on the preservation of liberty in the State and the maintenance of stable popular government which commanded the admiration of Macaulay, and to which the political theory of the Whigs was very considerably indebted. As secretary to the Florentine Republic, Machiavelli had learnt to believe in maintaining a safe political equilibrium by a series of checks and balances. In the words of Jacob Burckhardt, to examine a plan of his drafting is like looking into the works of a clock. In political theory, therefore, he was one of the first to emphasize the value of conflicting interests in the State, so that one may hold the other in check. " In every republic," he wrote, " there are two different dispositions, that of the populace and that of the upper class . . . all legislation favourable to liberty is brought about by the clash between them." From this and other reflections of the kind it might be argued that Machiavelli, not the devil, was the first Whig.

He can certainly claim to have been the first exponent of utilitarian political theory. The doctrine of the greatest good of the greatest number appears by implication in his political writings and is formulated in almost those words in, of all his works, that ribald little comedy *Mandragola*. It is curious to reflect that the sage formula of Bentham and James Mill was first used to justify a seduction.

In the latter half of the nineteenth century resurgent Italy, looking about for heroes, selected Machiavelli as an early prophet of national unity. His disgust with the ineptitude of Italian petty politics certainly led him to say things which can be so interpreted. He believed in a strong, efficient State and regretted the corruption and enslavement of his country which had been brought about by the quarrelsome inefficiency of its princes and republics. Moreover, like the good public servant he had been, he believed that men should make sacrifices for the common weal. In the passages where he commends the nobility for public spirit, of which the Roman republic could offer such heroic examples, his writing glows with an unusual fervour. Partly on account of these, and still more because of his love for Italy, the greatest of his biographers, Villari, hailed him as the " least understood and most calumniated personality that history has known." He even went so far as to add that Machiavelli's burning hope for a free Italy crowned his brows, " with a divine splendour that glorifies the age."

The heyday of nationalism and *Realpolitik* was evidently the moment for Machiavelli's triumphant return from the Inferno to which the Counter-Reformation had banished him and the limbo of reputation in which he had remained ever since. His sincere belief in a strong united State appealed to the nationalist, and his acute observation of facts to the realist. The moment has passed. His nationalism no longer pleases a generation which has suffered too much from aggressive nations. His glorification of the single-minded civic virtue which sacrifices private interest and private moral standards to the superior needs of the State has an ugly sound to those who have seen the oppression of Leviathan at its worst, whether in his own Italy or elsewhere. His realism appears academic in an age when politics no longer seem to depend on those more or less direct problems of personal decision which figure so largely in Machiavelli's statecraft, but rather on social and economic forces obscurely apprehended and hard to control. There is, moreover, too much in his writing to sicken and dismay. His most ardent admirers cannot deny that he advocates both craft and cruelty as legitimate weapons in statecraft. It is true that he insists that neither should be used for itself alone. It is true that he regards their use as inevitable, given the depravity of man, and fences all his doctrines with the specious plea that statesmen must live as the world lives. The service he hoped to do humanity—and he sincerely believed that he was serving humanity—was that of teaching the wicked to be wicked reasonably, or at least to achieve reasonable and reputable ends by reasonable if disreputable means.

No honest historian can deny that the epochs during which high moral purpose has played a large part in politics have been as disordered and unhappy as those in which it has not. The righteous ruler has not, in practice, necessarily been the best for his people. On the other hand, he has not necessarily been worse or less successful than the unrighteous, nor have epochs of realist and amoral politics been markedly superior in their results to the others. The facts prove nothing, or anything. In the circumstances righteousness might perhaps be given the benefit of the doubt. Examples can be cited in which firmness of moral judgment has triumphed over political wisdom, although Machiavelli cites none. This is the weakness of the Machiavellian method. His claim to objectivity is false. It is false because his admiration for the vanished Roman past controlled and limited his vision, and it is false because his natural taste for subtlety, and his admiration for cleverness and force directed his choice of historical examples.

The real flaw lies in the application of his method to a type of material—historical evidence—which ought not to be treated in this way. Its very nature prevents objective observation. The selection of examples and the kind of conclusions drawn from them is essentially personal. The interpretation of historical facts differs radically from the interpretation of natural phenomena because the same fact does not appear in the same light to any two observers and the relative importance, or even the notice, accorded to individual facts differs with the judgment and character of every historian. Thus Machiavelli's discovery of a method which was later to be valuable when applied to the natural sciences was made in a branch of knowledge where it was liable to be misleading and dangerous. Since his time the practice of assuming general laws from selected historical facts has been practised by hundreds without the tenth part of his dexterity or percipience. It is possible that his most harmful legacy to the modern world is this fallacious practice of arguing to supposed general principles from the insecure and imperfectly apprehended premises which are all that history has to offer.

# LITERATURE AND THE HISTORIAN

THE MODERN historian is compelled by all the influences of the time to approach literature with a certain diffidence. On the one side he hears the echoes of those warnings uttered by scholars against the delusions of fine writing and the cultivation of history as an art. He may uneasily recall the statement of that great and human scholar J. B. Bury that 'history is a science, neither more nor less,' or the dictum of Professor York Powell in his inaugural lecture at Oxford in the 1890's that 'style has no more to do with history than it has with law or astronomy.'

On the other side he may feel the silent reservations of his fellow writers, the poets, the novelists, the literary critics, and sometimes of the public. For history, by comparison, appears uncreative, the fruit rather of study than of inspiration. Dr. Johnson declared that 'in historical composition all the greatest powers of the human mind are quiescent . . . there is no exercise of invention. Imagination is not required in any high degree.'

The historian can, however, take heart from the undeniable fact that history had a secure place among the muses from classical antiquity, which was not seriously questioned until after the scientific revolution of the seventeenth and eighteenth centuries: a revolution which, in western Europe, so thoroughly shook up men's ideas and values that equilibrium has never fully been regained.

If he has the good fortune to write in English he can further seek reassurance in contemplating that long alliance between history and literature which has been, and still is, one of the glories of the English-speaking peoples. The tradition stretches back five centuries past Gibbon, Clarendon, Bacon, Raleigh, to the Berners translation of Froissart: it has been upheld and renewed in the twentieth century on both sides of the Atlantic.

It is a tradition distinguished by writing of many different kinds—vivid narrative and lucid exposition, dramatic projection of character, or reflective analysis. The English language has many moods and the historian makes use of them all.

I should like to call a few passages to mind, but with this warning—that of all prose, historical prose lends itself least well to this process of selection. History being the record of human action is a richly variegated material, and it is not easy to give a true impression of the stuff by snipping off an inch or two for a pattern.

Here none the less are some passages. First a piece of direct narrative from Berners's translation of Froissart describing Wat Tyler's march on London—surely one of the best accounts of a popular rising ever written, so fearful in its straight simplicity.

"In the morning on Corpus Christi day, King Richard heard mass in the Tower of London, and all his lords, and then he took his barge with the Earl of Salisbury, the Earl of Warwick, the Earl of Oxford and certain knights, and so rowed down along the Thames to Rotherhithe whereas was descended down the hill a ten thousand men to see the King and to speak with him. And when they saw the King's barge coming they began to shout and make such a cry, as though all the devils of hell had been among them . . . And when the King and his lords saw the demeanour of the people, the best assured of them were in dread; and so the King was counselled by his barons not to take any landing there but so rowed up and down the river. And the King demanded of them what they would, and said how he was come thither to speak with them, and they said all with one voice: 'We would that you should come a-land and then we shall show you what we lack.' Then the Earl of Salisbury answered for the King and said: 'Sirs, ye be not in such order or array that the King ought to speak with you.' And then the King was counselled to return again to the Tower of London and so he did.

" And when these people saw that, they were inflamed with ire and returned to the hill where the great band was, and there showed them what answer they had and how the King was returned to the Tower of London. Then they cried all with one voice, 'Let us go to London', and so they took their way thither; and in their going they beat down abbeys, and houses of advocates and men of the court, and so came into the suburbs of London which were greater and fair and there beat down diverse fair houses . . . There were many within the city of their accord, and so they drew together and said 'Why do we not let these good people enter into the city? They are our fellows, and that they do is for us.' So therewith the gates were opened and then these people entered into the city and went into houses and sat down to eat and drink. They desired nothing but it was incontinent brought to them, for every man was ready to make them good cheer and to give them meat and drink to appease them."

Now, to leap the centuries, and try a different manner and a different subject, here is Macaulay's dramatic portrait of Thomas Wentworth, Earl of Strafford:

" But Wentworth—whoever names him without thinking

of those harshly dark features, ennobled by their expression into more than the majesty of an antique Jupiter; of that brow, that eye, that cheek, that lip wherein, as in a chronicle, are written the events of many stormy and disastrous years, high enterprise accomplished, frightful dangers braved, power unsparingly exercised, suffering unshrinkingly borne; of that fixed look, so full of severity, of mournful anxiety, of deep thought, of dauntless resolution, which seems at once to forbode and to defy a terrible fate, as it lowers on us from the canvas of Van Dyck? . . .

" He was the first Englishman to whom a peerage was a sacrament of infamy, a baptism into the communion of corruption. As he was the earliest of that hateful list, so was he also by far the greatest; eloquent, sagacious, adventurous, intrepid, ready of invention, immutable of purpose, in every talent which exalts or destroys nations pre-eminent, the lost Archangel, the Satan of the Apostasy . . ."

Differences in style reveal differences in temperament; after the generous heat of Macaulay the cool irony of Edward Gibbon:

" It is a very honourable circumstance for the morals of the primitive Christians, that even their faults, or rather errors, were derived from an excess of virtue. The bishops and doctors of the Church, whose evidence attests, and whose authority might influence, the professions, the principles, and even the practice of their contemporaries, had studied the scripture with less skill than devotion and they often received, in the most literal sense, those rigid precepts of Christ and the apostles to which the prudence of succeeding commentators has applied a looser and more figurative mode of interpretation. Ambitious to exalt the perfection of the gospel above the wisdom of philosophy, the zealous fathers have carried the duties of self mortification, of purity and of patience, to a height which it is scarcely possible to attain, and much less to preserve in our present state of weakness and corruption. A doctrine so extraordinary and so sublime must inevitably command the veneration of the people; but it was ill calculated to obtain the suffrage of those worldly philosophers who, in the conduct of this transitory life, consult only the feelings of nature and the interest of society."

To come to the present century, here is G. M. Trevelyan in the mature manner of his social history, which never approaches the cynicism of Gibbon. He is describing the manners of the early eighteenth century:

" It was the privilege of all gentlemen, from a Duke downwards, to wear swords, and to murder one another by rule. As soon as men were well drunk of an evening they were apt to quarrel, and as soon as they quarrelled they were apt to draw their swords in the room, and if manslaughter was not committed on the spot, to adjourn to the garden behind the house, and fight it out that night with hot blood and unsteady hand. If the company were not wearing swords, the quarrel might be slept upon and forgotten or arranged in the sober morning. The wearing of swords, though usual in London, as being like the full-bottomed wig a part of full dress, was fortunately not common in the depths of the country among the uncourtly but goodnatured rural squires, whose bark was often worse than their bite. And even at Bath, Beau Nash employed his despotic power to compel the fashionable world to lay aside their swords when they entered his domain: in this he did as good service to the community as in teaching the country bumpkins to discard their top boots and coarse language at the evening assemblies and dances. During his long supremacy as Master of the Ceremonies, nearly covering the reigns of Anne and the first two Georges, Nash did perhaps as much as any other person even in the Eighteenth Century to civilize the neglected manners of mankind."

Last of all, here is another portrait in the grand manner, from a living writer:

" There now appeared upon the ravaged scene an Angel of Deliverance, the noblest patriot of France, the most splendid of her heroes, the most beloved of her saints, the most inspiring of all her memories, the peasant Maid, the ever shining, ever glorious Joan of Arc. In the poor remote hamlet of Domremy, on the fringe of the Vosges Forest, she served at the inn. She rode the horses of travellers, bare back, to water. She wandered on Sundays into the woods, where there were shrines and a legend that some day from these oaks would arise one to save France. In the fields where she tended her sheep the saints of God, who grieved for France, rose before her in visions. St. Michael himself appointed her, by right divine, to command the armies of liberation. Joan shrank at first from the awful duty, but when he returned attended by St. Margaret and St. Catherine, patronesses of the village church, she obeyed their command. There welled in the heart of the Maid a pity for the realm of France, sublime, perhaps miraculous, certainly invincible . . ."

That of course, is from Sir Winston Churchill's *History of the English-Speaking Peoples*.

The literary achievement is splendid, but in spite of all, the chill of scholarly criticism strikes to the bone. It cannot be denied that the literary historians are open to criticism for failures of perception and failures of scholarship which can at times be traced directly to their literary technique. Macaulay's denunciation of Strafford is noble in sound and volume, inspired in its range of images. But, by striking off so splendid a phrase as 'the Satan of the Apostasy', Macaulay introduced a Miltonic grandeur into our vision of the man and the epoch, which makes it hard to bring the mind down again to the sober and pedestrian level on which alone historical inquiry can be safely pursued, and just estimates made of persons and things.

I would not willingly forgo Macaulay's splendid phrase, but a great power over words and images can and does intoxicate, and the historian has chosen a branch of literature in which the utmost sobriety is usually advisable. It is not quite always advisable because there is the delicate and subtle problem of historic imagination: the power to move, or to give the impression of moving, from one epoch into another, the capacity to feel and think the thoughts of another time. This is a gift of literary imagination, and at its highest it sometimes resembles a state, if not of intoxication, then of possession. Thomas Carlyle is more frequently and more strenuously possessed by this kind of imagination than any other British historian. He ceases to be a recorder of the scene and becomes himself an actor, or more truly a disembodied spirit, restlessly moving from the mind of one character to another. He makes nothing of travelling two hundred years on the thunderclouds of his imagination to give a helping hand to Cromwell and his men at the Battle of Dunbar.

" The night is wild and wet . . . the Harvest Moon wades deep among clouds of sleet and hail. Whoever has a heart for prayer, let him pray now, for the wrestle of death is at hand. Pray,—and withal keep his powder dry! And be ready for extremities, and quit himself like a man! . . . the hoarse sea moans bodeful, swinging low and heavy against those whinstone bays; the sea and the tempests are abroad, all else asleep but we,—and there is ONE that rides on the wings of the wind.

" About four o'clock comes order to my pudding headed Yorkshire friend, that his regiment must mount and march straightway . . . Major Hodgson riding along heard, he says, ' a Cornet praying in the night'; a company of poor men, I think, making worship there, under the void Heaven, before battle joined; Major Hodgson turned aside to listen for a minute and worship and pray along with them; haply his last prayer on Earth, as it might prove to be. But no . . . the Heavens in their mercy I think have opened us a way of deliverance!—The Moon gleams out, hard and blue, riding among hail clouds; and over St. Abb's Head, a streak of dawn is rising . . . The Scots too . . . are awake; thinking to surprise us; there is their trumpet sounding, we heard it once; and Lambert who was to lead the attack is not here. The Lord General is impatient; behold Lambert at last! The trumpets peal, shattering with fierce clangour Night's silence; the cannons awaken along all the line: ' The Lord of Hosts! The Lord of Hosts!' On, my brave ones, on!' "

It is difficult to be sure whether the Lord General, who leads these praying troops to victory at the first streak of dawn after a stormy night, is in truth Oliver Cromwell, or a renegade Scot called Thomas Carlyle. The imaginative leap is complete. Carlyle has written himself and thought himself into the very heart of the scene. Without this extraordinary achievement of personal projection, English history as well as English literature would be the poorer for what is, by and large, a masterly interpretation of the Puritan mind in general and of Oliver Cromwell in particular.

But such imaginative fervour can be very unsafe; the slightest slip in scholarship makes it at once appear ridiculous. It is the measure of Carlyle's greatness that, although he did make mistakes, he emerges none the less as one of the great masters. But the dangers of his method, in these days of more searching scholarship, are apparent. The writer who trusts too deeply in his imaginative powers to recreate the past falls into an error as dangerous and more ridiculous than the writer who resists the imaginative impulse altogether.

Exuberance of imagination, whether about words or phrases or the interpretation of the past, can betray the writer into exaggerations and errors when he is working within the strict limits of history. On the other hand, the measured and restricted manner, the urbane, well-bred style of Edward Gibbon for instance, is not fitted to illuminate the darker or the higher reaches of the human spirit or to give more than a brilliant surface account of their manifestations. The *Decline and Fall* is the greatest masterpiece of historical writing in the English language; there are moments at which that clear, emphatic, and witty style stands between the author and the full interpretation of his subject. Gibbon's style, which reflects his mind, forces him to make light of things too complicated and too illogical or too sublime to be accommodated in the balanced framework of his sentences. But much of history, and much of human thought, is complicated and illogical, and some of it is sublime.

There is no literary style which may not at some point add to or take away something from the ascertainable outline of truth, which it is the task of scholarship to excavate and re-establish. The ability to light upon a splendid phrase, the imaginative power to breathe life into the names and actions of people long dead, may be misleading in one way; the clear, logical, and moderated manner, the epigrammatic, the concise, and the witty, may be as misleading in another.

It was partly, though not entirely, because the literary historians could sometimes be shown to have sacrificed the demands of scholarship to the demands of style that an open antagonism to literary treatment grew up among historical scholars in the later nineteenth century. Hence the dictum that style has no more to do with history than with law or astronomy. A gentler compromise was reached by Sir Charles Firth when he argued that the clear presentation of history is a necessary part of the historian's work; some art, he declared, was essential to this task and should be cultivated. History could not stand alone as a pure science. This point of view, modified by the temperamental leanings of individuals towards science or towards art, is now fairly generally held by academic historians.

The relationship of science to art in history is admitted; but the exact nature of that relationship remains undefined and possibly indefinable. Is literature the constant helpmeet and partner of scholarship, or is it the poor relation asked down for a few days once a year to assist at some necessary social occasion and help to hand round the drinks? Is the literary presentation of his work something which only begins to concern the historian when the work of scholarship is done, or is it something always present to his mind?

This problem can best be answered by negative arguments. The reaction against literature was mistaken and harmful, but it was not unreasonable or causeless. The great popular success of certain works of history which were, and are, also works of literature created a popular demand for history which was satisfied—had to be satisfied, the laws of supply and demand being what they are—by writers and historians of lesser value than those who had created the demand. The genius of a

Truth and Opinion

Macaulay, the vision of a J. R. Green are not given to everyone. Moreover it is a commonplace in all the arts, not in literature alone, that the style of a master, copied, diffused, ultimately parodied by imitators, can damage the reputation of the master and the art in question. Macaulay was well aware of this: ' My manner, is I think, and the world thinks, on the whole a good one,' he wrote, ' but it is very near to a bad manner indeed, and those characteristics of my style which are most easily copied are the most questionable.' The same could be said of Gibbon, whose manner, badly imitated, had a stultifying effect on English historical style for generations. In our own time, in the narrower field of biography, the imitators of Lytton Strachey managed by their smart-aleck antics to obscure for a long decade what was really valuable in the new approach to biography.

When bad popular work came flooding in to fill the demand created by good work it was not remarkable that the more austere and conscientious historians revolted against the popular treatment of history, and came not to distinguish very clearly between popular history and literary history. The revolt against the literary treatment of history was really a revolt against popularization, in which writers of vision and power were indiscriminately condemned, along with their inferior imitators.

Furthermore, history has followed the same curve during the last two to three generations as many other branches of knowledge. First a great increase in available information and evidence led to the development of new and more precise techniques of research. Then technical advances and ever-widening fields of inquiry led to over-confidence in man's capacity to attain exact knowledge. This was followed by the dismaying discovery that men know less by knowing more. A profusion of evidence means conflicting evidence. By and large, over the whole field, doubt and uncertainty increase with the increase of information.

The flow and meaning of events, the relation of cause to effect are no longer clear. Historians have dug out information about the structure of society or its economic foundations, the physical conditions or the spiritual preoccupations of our forefathers, which modify or revolutionize, or merely confuse, the once accepted versions of the past. Scholars of great perception and integrity disagree fundamentally on the construction to be put on the always increasing evidence available. What we once thought was progress, we are now constrained to regard as regress. In the interpretation of certain epochs, and indeed in our attitude to the whole story of man, we scarcely know any more if we are coming or going. When a philosopher historian of the scope and vision of Professor Toynbee arises to suggest an overall pattern, the specialist scholars, who are writhing like Laocoon in the toils of their more detailed research, wrench themselves free of their devouring doubts for just long enough to shoot him as full of arrows as Saint Sebastian.

Historical thinking is slowly and painfully going through very much the same process of questioning, destruction, and ultimate enlightenment that fell upon the natural sciences three hundred years ago. The old certainties are gone, the new are uncreated.

When so much is to be done and so much seems at stake— for we all have to believe that our own particular interest is of great importance to the world—is it to be wondered at that the mere creation of literature, this apparently irrelevant additional element in the historian's task, should seem of lesser importance to the research student, and the exact relationship of literature to history be left undefined?

It is only fair to the historian of today to remember that he thinks and works against this background of shifting values, of fluid knowledge and fluid opinions. This is very different from the atmosphere of more definite opinions, more rigid moral standards, and much more limited historical knowledge against which the classics of literary history were produced in the past.

The reaction against literary history was not causeless. Scholars had some grounds for thinking that historians with a strong literary gift were betrayed at times into sacrificing exactitude of statement to beauty of language, to minimizing or enhancing the historic picture by the qualities of individual style.

This is true. But the converse is not true. The historian who cultivates literary style can make mistakes, but there is no opposite guarantee that the historian with no literary style will make none. That is the great fallacy. Good writing is no guarantee of good scholarship; but neither is bad writing. The austere instinct which prompted the historians of fifty years ago to concentrate exclusively on discovery and regard the cultivation of writing as irrelevant, was a wrong instinct. There have been scholars of great distinction and valuable influence, who were bad writers. But they are rare. The sense of form, the capacity to weigh and to use words correctly, the shaping of sentences, and the structure and presentation of a scene, a fact, or an exposition are the natural concomitants of the clear, inquiring, disciplined, and imaginative mind which is needed for historical research. But most talents are the better for cultivation. The scholar who cultivates—as he must—the patience, the self-discipline, the spirit of inquiry, the open mind, the exactitude, and the strong but controlled imagination which are all necessary for research, will almost certainly find some of these qualities—equally important for the writer—reflected in his handling of the English language when he comes to set down his conclusions. In the same way, the writer who cultivates these qualities in his writing will find his perceptions sharpened and his ideas clearer when he turns to research.

74

J. B. Bury, who so sternly proclaimed that history was 'a science, neither more nor less', wrote himself with lucidity, ease, and distinction. The gritty, awkward and disjointed manner which marred a good deal of serious historical writing in the early years of this century frequently reflects the slow-moving, awkward, and short-sighted approach of the writers, not only to the beauties and possibilities of the English language but to the possibilities and beauties of historical inquiry. The close relationship between clear thinking and good writing is illustrated time and again by the work of the great scholars. This fact has been obscured by the common confusion between literary history and popular history. Properly speaking, all history which is written with style and distinction belongs to English literature; it need not necessarily be 'popular' in the sense that millions can read and understand it. In other branches of literature, the universal genius who speaks to all hearts and all ages, who does not become obscure by reason of contemporary allusions or turns of phrase that reflect passing fashions, is very rare—a Shakespeare, a Tolstoy. But no one would expect millions to read and appreciate the poems of John Donne, or the prose of C. M. Doughty. These are more specialized tastes; but such writing belongs none the less to the great heritage of literature.

In history alone the term "literary" has associations with the idea of popularity. It is assumed that good writing in history will occur most often, if not exclusively, in history which is directed towards a large public. But this does not follow. Much of the best historical writing of the last fifty years —and that in spite of the self-denying ordinance against literature passed by some of the practitioners themselves—has come from scholarly specialists, with little or no interest in reaching a large public or being acclaimed as literary figures. For the expressive, explicit, and exact use of words you would go far to find the equal of F. W. Maitland writing on the development of English law and institutions fifty years ago; and in this field today the great scholars, medieval or modern, Sir Maurice Powicke, Sir Lewis Namier have a precision, elegance, and clarity in the exposition of their themes which make many popular historians look slapdash and slipshod.

Anyone interested in modern English style would do well to turn, from time to time, away from the avowedly literary works, be they novels or criticism or literary history or that great field for fine writing so popular today, the travel book, and look into the pages of the learned periodicals. The subjects may be unappealing to the general reader but the manner in which they are treated is often an example of good style—cool, clear, reflective, and economical—in striking contrast to the average of modern popular writing, with its slack structure, careless and inattentive use of metaphors and images, and vocabulary corrupted by the stale-picturesque.

The practice of the finest scholars bears out the thesis that literature and scholarship, so far from being radically opposed to each other, are natural allies. Literary sensibility and literary technique are something more than pleasing additional graces to be cultivated by the historian if and when he has time. They are valuable to him not only in his final task of communicating his thoughts to the reading public, but from the very inception of his work; they will guide, help, and illuminate the whole process of historical inquiry.

The literary treatment of history is not a superficial thing; it goes to the root of the subject. Admittedly, it has its superficial aspects. For instance, the literary historian will often take note of superficial details which are irrelevant to the march of events and which would be rightly disregarded by a scholar dealing with, say, the evolution of ministerial responsibility or the fluctuations of wages in the fifteenth-century woollen industry. The literary historian will almost automatically make a note of any authentic details he can discover which are likely to enhance the reality of what he is describing or help the inward eye of the reader: the colour of a general's cloak or a woman's hair, the brightness or dullness of the weather, the hangings on the wall, the flowers in the garden—all things of very little consequence in themselves. In this respect the literary treatment of history is indeed merely an innocent and pleasing additional elegance. But this elegance can be used with wonderful skill and imagination, as for instance in Lytton Strachey's famous account of the dying Queen Victoria.

" Yet, perhaps, in the secret chambers of consciousness, she had her thoughts too. Perhaps her fading mind called up once more the shadows of the past to float before it and retraced for the last time the vanished visions of that long history—passing back and back, through the cloud of years, to older and ever older memories, to the spring woods at Osborne so full of primroses for Lord Beaconsfield—to Lord Palmerston's queer clothes and high demeanour, and Albert's face under the green lamp, and Albert's first stag at Balmoral, and Albert in his blue and silver uniform, and the Baron coming in through a doorway, and Lord M. dreaming at Windsor with the rooks cawing in the elm trees, and the Archbishop of Canterbury on his knees in the dawn, and the old King's turkey-cock ejaculations, and Uncle Leopold's soft voice at Claremont, and Lehzen with the globes, and her mother's feathers sweeping down towards her, and a great old repeater watch of her father's in its tortoise-shell case, and

77

a yellow rug, and some friendly flounces of sprigged muslin, and the trees and the grass at Kensington."

Here the details are accurate visual details assembled from many sources; slight in themselves, they have been selected, organized, and related to the story of the dying Queen in such a way as to illuminate what the author felt to be the essentials of her life and personality. Strachey's treatment can be compared with another closing passage, equally famous, written sixty years earlier—Motley's last lines on William the Silent.

"He went through life bearing the load of a people's sorrows upon his shoulders with a smiling face. Their name was the last word upon his lips, save the simple affirmative with which the soldier who had been battling for the right all his lifetime commended his soul in dying 'to his great Captain, Christ'. The people were grateful and affectionate, for they trusted the character of their 'Father William', and not all the clouds which calumny could collect ever dimmed to their eyes the radiance of that lofty mind to which they were accustomed, in their darkest calamities, to look for light. As long as he lived, he was the guiding star of a brave nation, and when he died the little children cried in the streets."

This passage from Motley's *Rise of the Dutch Republic* illustrates a further, and more significant, stage in the marriage between literary or æsthetic sensibility and historical enquiry. In the passage about the death of Queen Victoria, Strachey has selected from the thousands of small background details that he had accumulated about his subject a striking few that light up, here and there, the personal experiences of the Queen's lifetime. He is giving us here not history but conjecture based on historical knowledge; he is making, with considerably greater discretion

78

and restraint, the imaginative leap that Carlyle made at the Battle of Dunbar.

Motley does not depart from the stricter historical treatment of his theme. He conjectures nothing as to the state of William the Silent's mind in his last moments; he tells the facts and he sums up the impression objectively from contemporary evidence. Yet his summing up, like Strachey's more frankly imaginative flight, has the effect of poetry, the effect of striking through the surface facts to some deeper, less expressible truth about life and death and politics and the human heart.

The secret of Motley's great passage lies most of all in that last sentence: 'As long as he lived he was the guiding star of a brave nation, and when he died the little children cried in the streets.' The first part of the sentence is almost rhetorical, a sentence very well fitted to the old-fashioned idea of the dignity of history with its 'guiding star' and 'brave nation'—fine words but generalized and not particular to Motley or to the occasion; it is the last sentence, with its entirely simple statement of fact—' and when he died the little children cried in the streets' —which like a sudden beam of sunset light through clouds, streaming over the landscape, illuminates the whole of the preceding passage and tells us more about William the Silent as a ruler and as a leader than many piled-up paragraphs.

It has this effect because it is not a *rhetorical* phrase but an *historical* phrase; by the time the reader has got so far with Motley's *Dutch Republic* he knows his author well enough to understand that this is no flourish but a documented fact. He need not even consult the footnote to be reassured that these children were actually seen by someone walking in the streets of Delft at the time.

But—and this is the crux of the matter—this particular detail in a contemporary letter *might* have been missed by an historian less sensitive than Motley to æsthetic and literary values. The documentation of the epoch is very rich; there is a great deal to read and to digest; and in the mass of material it is not easy to hit upon the significant detail. By the significant detail I mean something much more than the picturesque detail. It is a superficial gift, though a useful one, to be able to pick out the vivid additional stage directions that may be found among the evidence—the picturesque touches. But it is a gift of a deeper kind to seize unfailingly on the kind of detail which illuminates to the core of an event. This is in part a literary gift, or rather it arises from the sharpening of perception which comes from literary training and the study and appreciation of literature.

It is not only in detail that the study and appreciation of literature, and the constant practice of history as an art, can be helpful to history as a science. The writer who approaches his task with some conception of the value and significance of form in writing or—more elementary still if you like—some idea of the sequence and flow of words and thoughts, some natural feeling for the relationship of words to form, will not fall into the danger of heaping up facts, and making a narrow, dry, unilluminating catalogue instead of an interpretation of his subject. If he has always in his mind a consciousness of the necessity of linking his material together, he will be a better historian as well as a better writer, for the problem of historical interpretation is largely a problem of finding out and establishing the correct relationships between facts; of restoring sequences of cause and effect whether in the lives of individuals or in much broader connections. In all this, the sense of form and structure, which has to be cultivated by the writer, is of equal importance to the historian.

The contention is one which cannot perhaps be proved except by negative evidence. History which is unimpeachable as scholarship should have lasting value regardless of its quality as writing. But when we look at the great works of scholarship which have lasted it is astonishing how rare it is to find one that reveals a writer devoid of literary skill and judgment.

Style in history is an index to the mind, and the great scholar, whether he cultivates it or not, is rarely without the natural gift. Fine writing may be the business only of the historian who has chosen to write of wide themes for a wide public. But good writing is almost the concomitant of good history. Literature and history were joined long since by the powers which shaped the human brain; we cannot put them asunder.

# ART, TRUTH AND HISTORY

T HE CONNECTION between art and truth, that is the apprehension of truth and its communication by means of art, is the central problem of every writer and of every creative artist. All writers are confronted with it, and take their own ways to solve it with greater or lesser success. Many writers have committed themselves to opinions about it in private letters or public statements which in their turn become the subject of further analysis and discussion by ensuing generations of writers and critics. The subject is inexhaustible. It presents questions which are of the utmost importance to the practising writer, and of scarcely less interest to the practising reader, that is the reader who takes his reading seriously and finds his pleasure enhanced by the sharpening of his critical faculties.

While it is true that the greatest art is to conceal art, and few admire writers who allow the mechanism behind their achievement to become visible, it is equally true that some appreciation of the technical skill of the artist deepens and enriches our pleasure. At the first impact of a beautiful poem or a great work of art we do not want to divert our minds by considering the ingenuity of vocabulary, the sensibility of hearing, the subtlety in the association of ideas which have brought together certain effects of sound, and stimulated certain trains of thought to create in us a spontaneous reaction of delight; so with a great picture we do not want consciously to notice at the first instant the deliberate touches by which the balance and harmony of line and colour have been produced; but at a second and third examination these things enhance our pleasure, because by recognizing the details of craftsmanship we make ourselves at second hand partners in the act of creation. Moreover, apart from this subtle self-flattery in which all critical readers secretly indulge, the education of the ear, the mind and the eye to detect and value the finer points does actually enhance the initial impact that a work of art has on us, because we are enabled to react more quickly and more fully to the writer's or the painter's intention.

For the historian, the relationship of art to truth is a particularly exacting one; it may even seem rather a narrow one. What more is there to be said but that the historian has to tell the truth? At least that is ideally what he is supposed to do, and some would say that art does not come into it at all. But art *does* come into it, for within the limitations of our human condition, truth is not apprehensible nor can it be communicated to another person without the help of art. To pass on any piece of information intelligibly requires a feat in the arrangement of words and ideas. Art may come in at an earlier stage, before that of communication. Simply to apprehend a fact intelligently and intelligibly requires a degree of art.

Benedetto Croce has equated art with intuition and argued that we cannot *know* anything until we have given it a name, that is—formalized it in our minds, and that this formalization, or naming is essentially a creative art. His English disciple, the philosopher and historian Collingwood, said that an historic fact only has meaning for us, in so far as we can re-think the thought that created it. The historian, according to Collingwood, has to make the creative act himself in the first place in his own mind. On the intensity with which he can make it depends the depth of his understanding of it. That is the first move: the first creative act. Only afterwards comes the second creative act of communication. On the skill with which he can communicate his thought depends his power to convey the meaning to others. They are two separate things and there is art in both.

This is not really any different from the processes of thought of any writer dealing with reality. It is what happens with the novelist or at least with those who deal in life as it is: not of course with the writers whose quality is a heightened imaginative power, the allegorical or the romantic, who illuminate life by lifting it into another atmosphere. But the creative writer, the novelist who aims at giving us life as it is, faces the same problem as the historian—the problem of reading the meaning of an incident and conveying it to the reader. Virginia Woolf wrote thus of Jane Austen:

" She makes us wonder why an ordinary act as she describes it becomes so full of meaning . . . Here is nothing out of the way. It is midday in Northamptonshire; a dull young man is talking to a rather weakly young woman on the stairs as they go up to dress for dinner, with housemaids passing. But from triviality, from commonplace, their words become suddenly full of meaning and the moment for both one of the most memorable in their lives. It fills itself; it shines; it glows; it hangs before us, deep, trembling, serene for a second; next, the housemaid passes, and this drop in which all the happiness of life has collected gently subsides again to become part of the ebb and flow of ordinary existence."

The incident comes from *Mansfield Park*. Edmund Bertram and Fanny Price are going upstairs on the eve of the ball given for Fanny; Edmund had only a few hours before planted in her bosom the seeds of anguish and ecstasy by coupling her and Mary Crawford as the 'two dearest objects I have on earth' and now in this incident on the stairs he assuages her agony by indicating that he has serious doubts of Mary Crawford's suitability as a wife.

But it is not only this moment, it is the whole extremely commonplace love story of Edmund and Fanny that Jane Austen irradiates, with never a false tone, simply by seeing the truth about these two dull virtuous young people with an artist's integrity and intensity. We cannot be amused and delighted by Fanny as we are by Emma Woodhouse and Elizabeth Bennett, because poor Fanny was not amusing or delightful, but we *know* her as if she were a living person, because Jane Austen has perfectly created and perfectly projected her. Fanny's experience first became a part of Jane Austen's experience and then a part of ours.

The historian has to do very much the same thing, with this difference; that the novelist is free to adapt and invent provided that the material is that of authentic and living experience. The historian, on the other hand, is dealing with events which once occurred independently of him and which he seeks to describe, or, if he is a pioneer, to re-establish accurately. But although everything about which the historian writes had at one time a separate existence in itself, it exists for him in the present only as he is able to re-think it. Thus the quality of our understanding of the past depends on the quality of understanding its interpreters have brought to it. The French Revolution was, at the time, a series of terrifying and present realities. Today it is a number of ideas and traditions, right or wrong, vague or vivid according to the intensity or accuracy with which the evidence has been examined and the ideas interpreted or transmitted.

The creative process of the artist in history is obvious enough in that kind of history which is generally called literary history —that is in history which is frankly designed to be read as literature. Literary history is concerned, and legitimately concerned, with conveying the writer's view of events to the reader with the greatest intensity. Many historians in the last two centuries have shown that history of this kind can also contain scholarship of great value. Several major works which were conceived and undertaken as works of literature and designed to appeal to the educated public as a whole were also works of significant and sometimes pioneer research. Gibbon's *Decline and Fall* embodies the most extensive scholarship; Motley's *Rise of the Dutch Republic* involved laborious and exhaustive work in the Dutch archives; Froude was the first historian to realise the necessity of consulting the Spanish archives and to penetrate into Simancas.

All histories conceived as literature have this in common; that they are written about subjects of general interest. They deal with people and principles which are generally understood, with incidents interesting and dramatic in themselves. But there are many subjects which have to be studied and which ought to be studied, but which no historian could or should wish to turn into literary history. The underlying mechanism of administration, the slow development of institutions, the intricate interlocking of economic and social facts, which must of necessity be studied in meticulous detail and infinite variety unless we are to be misled by facile generalizations—all these things are of the greatest importance in the study of history, but very few of them can be adequately or even honestly treated in an essentially literary manner. Writing about them is none the less an art, and a very difficult one; and some works on these highly unliterary subjects are most certainly literature.

Frederick Maitland is by some considered to be our greatest

historian; certainly no one would deny him a place on the heights. Quite apart from what he wrote about, he wrote a clear, spare, lively English which is a pleasure to read. But when in his great book *Domesday Book and Beyond* he set out to trace and delineate the legal ideas which bound together the rural society of England in the eleventh century, he was writing for the students of medieval history and of law to whom his ideas were originally delivered in the form of lectures; and he was writing for the same kind of public outside the lecture hall— for specialists, for people who had professional reasons to learn about such things. He was not thinking about the general reader, and he could not do so, because that would have compelled him to simplify too much and to explain things that, with his students, he could take for granted. But his book, all his books, are works of art, both for the vision which forms them and the lucid manner in which they are written.

In 1888 in a lecture at Cambridge, Maitland regretted that no History of English law had ever been written; the ' great man for the great book' had not yet appeared. In fact he had appeared; he was born in 1871, was a schoolboy at the time of Maitland's lecture and his name was William Holdsworth. His majestic *History of English Law* came out between 1903 and 1938 and is the most important book on English history to appear in this century. But Professor Holdsworth did not expect the literary world to receive his book with raptures (he would have been embarrassed if they had done so) and he did not design it to be read with effortless delight by the general reader. If he had done so he might have written a brilliant essay on English law, but it would not have been the great and authoritative book that it is, the mine for all future historians to dig in.

There are innumerable historical themes too detailed, too vast, too abstruse, too specialized to be suitable for literary treatment in the generally accepted sense of the word. Yet any book on such a subject, if it is to be valuable at all, must be a work of art. There must be behind it a strong and clear apprehension of reality, and there must be the power to convey it to the readers for whom it is intended.

This has more to do with form than with style. The distinction between style and form is not always clearly made in practice. Style is the surface manner of presentation, the use of words, the shaping of sentences and paragraphs; form is the structure underlying, the ground plan and conception of the book. It is certainly better if a historian has both, but he can, and often does, do without style. He cannot do without form, for if his writing is formless his book ceases to be art and ceases to be history—it becomes a mere catalogue of statements, dry insignificant bricks without mortar.

It is a pity, of course, to do without style because even with the most abstruse subjects clarity and crispness are a help to presentation. Maitland was a master of the cool short sentence, and, unobtrusively, of the right choice of adjectives when adjectives were called for. Because of the closely-knit argument and the nature of his subject matter it is not very easy to take out a single paragraph for quotation as an example. But here he is summing up, at the end of a passage on land tenure and legal terminology at the time of the Conquest. First he utters a few significant but not over-weighted general principles:

"We must not be in a hurry to get to the beginning of the long history of law. Very slowly we are making our way towards it. The history of law must be a history of ideas. It must represent, not merely what men have done and said, but what men have thought in bygone ages. The task of reconstructing ancient ideas is hazardous, and can only be

88

accomplished little by little. . . . Against many kinds of
anachronism we now guard ourselves. We are careful of
costume, of armour and architecture, of words and forms of
speech. But it is far easier to be careful of these things than
to prevent the intrusion of untimely ideas,"

if, he elaborates, we introduce anachronistic ideas——

" we shall be doing worse than if we armed Hengist and
Horsa with machine-guns or pictured the Venerable Bede
correcting proofs for the Press; we shall have built upon a
crumbling foundation. The most efficient method of protecting
ourselves against such errors is that of reading our history
backwards as well as forwards, of making sure of our middle
ages before we talk about the ' archaic ', of accustoming our
eyes to the twilight before we go out into the night."

The effect of the extremely simple metaphor at the end is very
striking, because he uses metaphor so sparingly that it comes with
a shock of novelty, though in fact his figure of ' going out into
the night ' is straightforward, even commonplace, in itself.

Surface style is something which strikes the reader immediately; it is what attracts us to, or repels us from, a writer in the
first place. It played a foremost part therefore in the now ancient
controversy between the academic and the literary historians.
Both sides put too much emphasis on style (as though this was
the only place in which a historian displayed his art) and this
caused a misapprehension of what was really meant by art, and
the consequent revolt of scholars against art at the close of the
last century. History they claimed was a science pure and
simple.

The ire of the academic historians was aroused by the personal idiosyncrasies, the charm, the wit, the passion, the sheer individual energy displayed by the great literary historians. They noted with disapproval the evident prejudices of Macaulay or Froude, and with—possibly—a certain *schadenfreude* the weakness in technical knowledge which caused Carlyle, for instance, in his *Oliver Cromwell* to be taken in by some outrageously faked documents. They rather illogically ascribed the errors which they detected in these historians to the treatment of history as art, by which they meant nothing more than attention to style.

J. R. Seeley, who was still Professor of Modern History at Cambridge when the young Trevelyan was a student, spoke sternly to him, as he tells us in *Clio: a Muse*, on exactly this point. Art, asserted Professor Seeley, had nothing whatever to do with history. He was conscientiously anxious to eradicate any misapprehension on this point from the mind of the young student who, being a great-nephew of Macaulay, might well have a dangerous family inheritance.

Professor Seeley applied his anti-art attitude with some vigour to his own style which is aggressively unpleasing; he dammed the flow of his sentences with obstructive subsidiary clauses; he made no attempt at clarity or cleanness of phrase, so that often his sentences have to be read several times before their meaning is clear, and he mixed up abstract and concrete ideas, a slackness to which historical writing is all too subject—as for instance: ' The Counter-reformation broke out ' as though the Counter-reformation were a wild beast in a cage.

Yet Seeley's two major historical works, *The Growth of British Policy* and *The Expansion of England* are still, if not generally read from end to end, at least frequently consulted, and the ideas which he put forward in them played an influential part both on the interpretation of our history and on our political ideas. This could not have been so unless he had been in some degree also an artist, whether he knew it or not. And undoubtedly he was, because he had a powerful sense of form. His style most certainly does not flow, but his ideas do, and once the reader has surmounted the surface difficulties he will find that Seeley's books have great persuasive power; because the facts are related to each other with discrimination and vision. It is not necessary to agree with his ultimate conclusions in order to admire the skill with which he amasses and arranges his knowledge to arrive at them. While vigorously repudiating the use of art as unfit for the science of history, he showed a high degree of artistic skill in his own treatment of his material.

I never had the honour to meet the late Sir William Holdsworth, the great historian of English law, but I should imagine he was not a man who had much patience with the airs and graces of literary history. Yet in the marshalling of his facts, the shaping of his argument, the interplay of narrative and analysis, the vision with which he relates the small particular incident to the general argument, the skill with which he distinguishes and analyses the many different forces at work in the shaping of English law, he is a major artist.

Those who proclaimed that history was a science pure and simple did no damage to literature but they did some damage to history. Writers are tough, and writers who wished to write history were bound to go on writing, whatever the academics said to discourage them. The damage was done not by discouraging writers, but by encouraging those who had no æsthetic gifts at all to believe that they could do very well in history in spite of this deficiency. But the card index is not knowledge. It is only the beginning of knowledge, and the accumulation of facts is useless until they are related to each other and seen in proportion. Historical material cannot be intelligently understood without a certain æsthetic sense. Sir

John Neale, who writes with equal success in both kinds of history—the literary and the academic—has said in one of his essays " All facts are not born free and equal," and indeed they are not. There is a hierarchy of facts. To arrange them rightly, to distinguish the important from the trivial, to see their bearing one upon another, requires a skill which is very comparable to that of the painter giving significant form to the objects before him, judging the values of light and shade, or the spatial dispositions of shape and colour.

The good historian, whatever his theme, must be an artist. Without art there may be accumulations of statements, there may be calendars or chronicles, but there is no history. Any way of thinking about, or looking at, historical facts, which has any value at all, must be an exercise of the imaginative and discriminating faculties. History in any intelligible form *is* art.

But if history is *art*, in what way does the historian's attitude to art and truth differ from that of the essentially imaginative writer? Very profoundly. It is the privilege and indeed the function of the creative artist to use, that is to manipulate and to intensify, the truth about life as he sees it. The bare truth is not enough in itself. " Realism by itself is fatal," said Turgenev, and, in another passage on the same subject " Truth is the air without which we cannot breathe, but art is a plant, sometimes even a rather fantastic one, which grows and develops in this air." It is self-evident that these are two statements that no historian should make, or even think. Realism is fatal? But the historian laboriously strives after the whole unvarnished truth. " Art is a plant, sometimes a fantastic one "—but the pedestrian historian cannot allow anything fantastic, except of course when the vagaries of human nature do really—as they sometimes do—produce a fantastic effect.

The letters and commonplace books of writers are full of

indications of the way in which experiences and incidents from life can be and must be adapted, expounded, telescoped, or amalgamated to make novels and stories, to make *literature*. Henry James evolves a situation from a fragment of conversation overheard at a tea party; Joyce Cary describes the face of a woman seen on a boat-trip, a visual memory, which was later vitalized by the fragment of a half-heard anecdote and from which grew a story which was only very tenuously related to the chances which inspired it.

The work of creative imagination is *controlled* by experience; it has to spring from knowledge and understanding of life, but the writer is free to use and reject what he wants, to present a heightened or simplified picture; he is not subservient to the facts he has accumulated or the observations he has made. They are his material to be freely used as his art directs, and he can invent or discard as it suits him.

The historian cannot do this. He can only use what he has before him. He cannot invent and—this may be even more difficult—he cannot reject except within very cautious limits. The novelist—and this goes for the historical novelist too—can reject those parts of the material which for one reason or another seem to add nothing to what he wishes to project. Indeed selection of essentials is an important part of his art. The historian can only select in a much more limited manner; naturally he *does* select and reject because everything cannot be included in an intelligible book. There must be some theme or theory, and there must be some parts of the historical material which are adjudged not relevant. But over-selection, over-simplification are major causes of misrepresentation in history, and the historian cannot ask with the novelist: does this fact add anything to the pattern of my novel as I see it? to the projection of this character or this situation as I intend it? He has to ask:

does this fact add anything to my knowledge and understanding of this incident, of this situation, of this epoch? And he must be very sure indeed that it adds nothing before he decides to pass it over.

The historian has to decide whether an apparently irrelevant fact is truly irrelevant. He also has to find a place for the awkward fact which does not fit with the pattern of development or the scheme of events as he had at first seen it. This is often a strain on his patience and his conscience. He has to find a place for new evidence which will make sense when added to the existing evidence, whether or not the result fits in with his own theories. If his theory is destroyed by new evidence, he must abandon it and start again. It is never safe and it is usually impossible to insert new material into the texture of an older theory. The attempt to do so produces a result like that picture of the Gerbier family which was begun by Rubens during his visit to England in 1630. Gerbier, an engraver, a go-between in the traffic in works of art, who was under the patronage of Charles I, had a handsome wife and a family of pretty, plump children whom Rubens painted when he was staying in their house. But the lady was very fruitful and had many more children later; new pieces of canvas were attached to the picture at one side and additional little Gerbiers, not by Rubens, were introduced. The effect is very strange, not only because the picture has an extra foot or two that does not fit, but because the original fluid and beautifully placed composition by Rubens has been thrown out of balance.

New material, new evidence, additional historical facts are very like the little Gerbiers. They should not be added on. A new picture has to be painted, a new composition thought out, which will include all the children, or all the facts, in a new relationship to each other.

But although the pattern, from the very nature of things, has frequently to be altered, there must be a pattern for the historical process to be apprehended at all. G. M. Young has said of the historian:

" Movement and continuity are the conceptions with which he works and what æsthetic writers claim a passionate apprehension of form to be to the painter, a passionate apprehension of process is to the historian."

This is true, but like all obsessions, the obsession with process can become dangerous. For when a highly satisfactory pattern of process has been worked out by the historian he is very unwilling to let it go; yet he may have to let it go if facts come to light which gravely modify it. Almost any theory about historical process could be sustained, almost any pattern could be worked out, if the historian allowed himself the freedom of other creative writers to eliminate what he does not wish to see. Being human, most historians do, to some extent, fall into this error, and some much more seriously than others.

The historian's sense of form should never be so strong that he cannot modify the shape into which he has cast his material when new evidence compels him to do so. It should never be so strong, but often is; and there are occasions when historians behave far more like writers of fiction than they either admit or know. There can be very few who have not at some time or other made an unconscious excision or elimination; or turned a blind eye to details which did not suit their books. It is a price that has to be paid, because without the sense of form there can be no capacity to relate facts, to analyse them, to compose or to sustain an argument. G. M. Young is right when he talks of the passionate apprehension of process; without passion in this sense who would undertake or carry through the backbreaking, eye-aching business of research, and count a hundred hours well spent if they produce one fragment of evidence, or one long-desired clue? Without passion there might be no errors; but without passion there would certainly be no history.

To raise once more the old question—is History an Art or a Science? Or is it as some have argued a hybrid between the two? The best answer is to turn the question inside out. All sciences are devoted to the quest for truth; truth can neither be apprehended nor communicated without art. History therefore is an art, like all the other sciences.

IN TWO senses it may be said that history embraces the whole of literature: first, because the creation of all literature occurs within the limits of history, and secondly, because all literature arises, directly or indirectly out of history, for all literature arises out of human experience and all human experience is potential history. The writer may treat his material in any number of different ways. He may express himself in romance or fantasy, in poetry, drama or satire. He may adapt and organize material copied from the world before him; he may soar into realms of speculation. Yet at some point every work of creative literature is attached, however slightly, to experience. At some point it must make contact with what we think of as reality— the observed world about us. A work of literature, were this not so, would be inconceivable. No human mind is capable of ideas which have not at their source some kind of human experience. History, rightly understood, includes the whole of human experience. Therefore, it may be argued that all literature is in this wide sense historical.

But our education and the idioms that we use, emphasize certain elements of experience as though they alone were historical. A statesman is described as having " made history " as though this were a special function of a statesman; or a nation is said to be " making history " when it becomes involved in some particularly violent or remarkable circumstances. But every human being is making history all the time. We live in history as we live in air and we cannot escape it.

History, in the narrower and generally accepted popular sense, has supplied subjects for a very great part of the drama, the poetry and the fiction of the world. Writers have taken up and simplified or embroidered some actual situation, some story whose principal characters were at least already outlined for them. Sometimes they have imbued such individual happenings with something of universal value. This use of historical material goes back a long time before the arrival of the self-conscious and sophisticated creative writer. It is one of the earliest and most natural tendencies of man to try to distil out of harsh facts a more poetic and universal meaning, to give them at once a quality of simplicity and permanence.

In the process of turning history into the simpler and pro-founder stuff of poetry it was sometimes found necessary, and therefore permissible, to adapt and alter the material. From this fusion of a little that was historic with much that was poetic sprang many of the great epics, the *Iliad* or the *Chanson de Roland*, the *romanceros* of Spain, the ballads of Scotland and much of the folk literature of the world. Until recently more sophisticated writers retained something of this natural freedom in adapting the facts of recorded, or remembered, history to their needs. In this age when we are by way of making a god of accuracy—and accuracy is not necessarily at all the same thing as truth—it is worth pausing for a moment to look at the effect of this, not on historians but on creative writers who are attracted towards history.

The extent to which a writer dares to modify the facts about which he decides to write depends on the conventions of his time. Schiller was perfectly at liberty to arrange a meeting between Mary Queen of Scots and Queen Elizabeth—a meeting which, if we are to be accurate in our history, never took place. But the liberties allowed to a modern dramatist or a modern novelist by a modern audience are not nearly so great because there is now considerable confusion in the public mind as to the purpose of the historical drama or novel—or for that matter the historical film. It tends to expect from them instruction in history as well as, or possibly even more than, æsthetic pleasure or mere entertainment. The modern writer therefore who wants to convey something more valuable than a little elementary historical instruction, and yet wants to use material taken from history, is compelled more or less strictly, to keep within the limits laid down by record.

It is instructive to notice how often in modern times a creative writer who is using historical material has to employ some different approach or some ingenious device when he wishes to emphasize the more profound message that he is seeking to convey. He has by this means to evade the possibility of purely pedantic criticism on the part of the public. Shaw in *St. Joan* transferred the whole of his last act to a dream, and in dreams all laws of realism can be suspended. Again T. S. Eliot in *Murder in the Cathedral* uses throughout a vocabulary and a technique which removes the drama from the solid earth of the twelfth century and lodges it essentially in the human soul which knows no chronology.

It was possible for Shakespeare, for Goethe, for Corneille, for Schiller, even for Victor Hugo, to use historical names as empty vials into which they could pour their own conceptions and so illuminate the passions, the weaknesses or the virtues of man. Shakespeare's Macbeth is not an exact portrait of a certain eleventh century King of Scotland but is a profound and illuminating study of a living and comprehensible man, weak, not without nobility, gradually corrupted by ambition. As such it has a value far superior to a more accurate portrait of the historic Macbeth. Schiller's *Don Carlos* is very definitely not an exact portrait of the eldest son of Philip II. But it is a most wonderfully moving and compassionate study of a young irresolute man, torn between conflicts which are too great for him. These and others like them, are great studies of human character. To ask whether they are true accounts of the people whose names they carry is irrelevant. The poetic truth is too effective to be challenged by mere historic truth.

It is a delicate and rather a dangerous thing for a historian to appear to attach only an inferior value to accuracy of statement about historical events and there are contexts in which the suggestion that poetic truth could be superior to historic truth might be dangerous. But these examples are not intended to prove that the creative writer has the right at all times and places to tamper with history. The rights and liberties which he is free to exercise in dealing with historical material vary with the conventions of his age, and liberties which are acceptable and fruitful at one time are no longer acceptable and therefore can no longer be fruitful at another. Yet whatever the present situation, it has been from very ancient times a natural and a healthy habit of mankind to poeticize and to simplify the most striking events of history: to modify individual historic truth into simple permanent forms. The creative artist may within the conventions of his epoch as legitimately use historical material in the same way.

As for the historian himself, if he has any ambition beyond that of amassing a mere catalogue of unrelated and therefore unintelligible statements, he must approach his material as any other creative artist does—with the sense that it contains some essential and permanent truths which it may be his skill or good fortune to release. It is with the character of those truths and with certain difficulties in approaching them that I am chiefly concerned.

The poet, the dramatist, the novelist are free to exercise their imagination as widely as they choose. But the historian may not be allowed so long a tether. He must fulfil his function as a creative artist only within very rigid limits. He cannot invent what went on in the mind of St. Thomas of Canterbury. The poet can. He cannot suppress inconvenient minor characters and invent others who more significantly underline the significance of his theme. The novelist can. The dramatist can. The historian, as Sir Philip Sidney has said, " is captive to the truth of a foolish world." Not only is he captive to the truth of a foolish world, but he is captive to a truth he can never fully discover, and yet he is forbidden by his conscience and his training from inventing it.

He gains his knowledge through evidence which, at the very best, is incomplete; which is always contradictory: which raises as many questions as it solves: which breaks off tormentingly just where he needs it most, or, yet more tormentingly, becomes ambiguous and dark. He can never establish the truth. He can only grope towards it; he gropes, moreover, with an intellect which, being furnished in the twentieth century, finds it extremely difficult to understand any other, which is over-confident, apt ·to leap to wrong conclusions, unaware of its own shortcomings or, if aware, then unable to make allowances for them. The greatest scholar can never reach more than some kind of partial and personal version of truth as it once was. All the efforts of historical scholarship are ultimately reduced to a mere matter of human opinion. In the preface to his *Civilization of the Renaissance in Italy* Jacob Burckhardt has somewhat discouragingly said:

> " In the wide ocean upon which we venture, the possible ways and directions are many and the same studies which have served for this work might easily in other hands not only receive a wholly different treatment but lead also to essentially different conclusions."

The painful predicament of the historian has never been better expressed. But it is important to remember that, in Burckhardt's mind this defeatist view was closely linked with another implicit assumption: that neither the uncertainty nor the personal nature of his own judgments exonerates the historian from applying the utmost of his critical faculties and scholarly abilities to establishing the truth, or the fact, according to his own lights. To do anything less is intellectual treason.

Surmounting the difficulties of discovering the truth about the historic facts, as far as in him lies, is a matter for the technical skill and conscience of each individual historian. It must be assumed of him, as of other writers, that he will have the self-respect to live up to what he considers the highest standards of his own profession. Historians certainly do commit deliberate dishonesties and, far more often, *bona fide* mistakes; there are as many blindnesses, perjuries, tergiversations, errors of judgment, blemishes of character, foibles, frailties, prejudices and shortcomings among historians as among any average group of mortals—or as among any average group of other writers for that matter.

None the less there are among historians a few who have from time to time cast as much light on the predicament of man as the free creative writers. There have been a few with as much insight into the human situation (within the limits allowed them), as much vision and compassion as the greatest writers outside the special bondage of history. But there is a terrible paradox inherent in the historian's profession which has done damage both to historians as writers and to society at large. The historian ought to be the humblest of men; he is faced a dozen times a day with the evidence of his own ignorance; he is perpetually confronted with his own humiliating inability to interpret his material correctly; he is, in a sense that no other writer is, in bondage to that material. Yet it is just precisely the historian among writers who is often the most arrogant. It is just precisely the historian who will often claim that he is not merely the master of his material but, by being the master and interpreter of the past, also the master of the future. It is just precisely among historians that the most conceited assumptions of knowledge, the most assured prophecies of the future, the most *ex cathedra* judgments of right and wrong will be found. On closer examination these judgments, these prophecies, these constructions of vast philosophies explaining the past, present and future of man will all prove to be rooted in the temporary political prejudice or philosophical beliefs of a particular historian or of a particular age or society. There have been among such philosophies and among such interpretations of history on a large scale, a few whose inherent nobility gave them a value of their own, not as history but as moral teaching. Great names from St. Augustine onwards shine out to redeem the noble error.

But it is an error. It is the great pitfall of history. The historian who forgets to be humble, who forgets the essentially inconclusive nature of his evidence and his own fallibility, who furthermore confuses the temporary opinions of a party or a nation or a religion with absolute standards of right and wrong, can unfortunately be very persuasive. He can take the petty developments of a few generations or a few centuries for some immutable law of progress; or imagine that the ephemeral rivalries of nations are in some way eternal and inevitable; or indulge half a dozen other aberrations. He may lead whole societies with him into error and make them act upon it.

The historian when he feels this powerful temptation, could take a lesson from the geologist. The Alps, for example, so majestically immutable as they seem, are to the geologist upstarts. They are a mere matter of thirty million years old. These youthful mountains, which came so late to their present shape and grandeur, show up the entire duration of recorded history for the wretched scantling of time that it is. From this little fragment, this few thousand years—about which we can never know more than the hundred-thousandth part and that uncertainly—historians have tried to construct systems and cycles of a scientific immutability. This is the minute kingdom over which, from time to time, a historian lords it as though he were the arbiter of the universe.

In pursuing such speculations, the historian is surely wrong— sometimes nobly wrong, sometimes foolishly so. The importance of history is not that of a science or a system; it is as a record of human beings, a source from which human experience can be studied. The purpose of this study is not to make general rules either political, economic or moral, but to get to the heart of the human problem. After several thousand years of experience in human society it is still the problem that we do not understand.

It can be justly argued that the historian's function is neither more nor less than that of any other creative writer. All literature arises from human experience and therefore all literature arises in the ultimate resort from historical material. The discipline and technique to which the historian submits his material is different from that of the imaginative writer. But the nature of his material is the same and the historian in so far as he stands or wishes to stand within the bounds of literature at all, has the same task as that of the creative artist. He is not to judge and prophesy and create systems, but within the limits allowed to him, to illuminate the human soul.

# EDWARD GIBBON

WHEN Edward Gibbon published the first volume of his *Decline and Fall of the Roman Empire* in 1776, it was hailed by the most eminent critic of his time as " a truly classic work ". In the hundred and eighty years which have elapsed since then, that contemporary judgment has been confirmed. Gibbon's great book is still read for pleasure and information. The balance and form of his presentation is as gratifying to the mind as a noble eighteenth-century building to the eyes. The flow of his narrative, the clarity of his prose and the edge of his irony still have power to delight and, although seven generations of scholars have added to or modified our knowledge of the epoch, most of what Gibbon wrote is still valid as history.

Edward Gibbon was born at Putney, then a pretty suburban village a few miles from London, in the year 1737. His father was a gentleman of extravagant habits and comfortable means with interests in the City; in his youth he and his family had come under the influence of William Law and his two sisters are said to appear in Law's *Serious Call* as the frivolous Flavia and the devout Miranda. The devout Miss Gibbon continued to be Law's disciple and a pillar of his holy household until his death in 1761. It is strange that so close a link should exist between the great mystical writer and the highly rational historian.

As a child Edward Gibbon was small and sickly, easily bullied by tougher boys at Dr. Wooddeson's school where he was sent at nine years old to learn Latin. Of the seven children born to his parents he alone survived, and his delicate mother died when he was ten, when he was handed over to the care of her sister, Catherine Porten. Nothing more fortunate could have happened to him, for this excellent woman combined all the qualities most necessary to his health and happiness. She was resourceful, energetic, practical, deeply affectionate, imaginative in her understanding of his intellectual needs and not unduly possessive. To ensure herself an independent income and to make a more cheerful home for her nephew, she set up a little boarding-house in London for boys attending Westminster—the school which Gibbon himself attended on the rare occasions when he was well enough to do so. He gained his real education from the wide general reading in which she encouraged him. In the autobiography which he carefully composed in later life he called her ' the true mother of my mind as well as of my health ' and left a grateful description of her personality: ' Her natural good sense was improved by the perusal of the best books in the English language and if her reason was sometimes clouded by prejudice, her sentiments were never disguised by hypocrisy or affectation. Her indulgent tenderness, the frankness of her temper, and my innate rising curiosity, soon removed all distance between us: like friends of an equal age we freely conversed on every topic, familiar or abstruse, and it was her delight and reward to observe the first shoots of my young ideas.'

In his twelfth year Gibbon describes himself as having fully developed that ' invincible love of reading, which I would not exchange for the treasures of India '. During the brief time that he was well enough to attend Dr. Wooddeson's school at Kingston he read Cornelius Nepos whose lucid simplicity he later commended as an excellent model. More important was his discovery of Homer in Pope's translation which, he says, 'accustomed my ear to the sound of poetic harmony'. In his mature style the influence of Pope's fluent precision in the use of words can still be traced. He read in the next two or three years everything on which he could lay hands—poetry, history, travel and romance—until in his own phrase his 'indiscriminate appetite subsided by degrees in the *historic* line'. He was fourteen when he came upon the *Universal History* while on a visit to friends and he 'was immersed in the passage of the Goths over the Danube when the summons of the dinner bell reluctantly dragged me from my intellectual feast'.

When he was sixteen his health suddenly improved; the prostrating headaches from which he had suffered as a child vanished away and he was sent to the University to complete his education. Owing to his irregular schooling and wide but unconventional reading he arrived at Oxford in 1752 with 'a stock of erudition which might have puzzled a doctor and a degree of ignorance of which a schoolboy might have been ashamed'. But so slack was the tuition at Oxford at that time that no one took the least notice either of his erudition or of his ignorance. Teaching and discipline were equally lax and Gibbon, who was ardent to acquire knowledge, was bored and disgusted. Thrown back on his resources during what he was later to call 'the most idle and unprofitable' months of his whole life, he began to examine the religious controversy recently caused by the publication of Middleton's *Free Enquiry into the Origin of Miracles*. The startling result of his researches into the early history of Christianity was his conversion to Catholicism, and he was privately received into the Church of Rome in June 1753.

As the law then stood in England, his conversion meant that he had to leave the University, and since Roman Catholics were excluded from public employment, it put a stop to any hope of a political or legal career. Gibbon's father, who was distressed at this unconventional turn in his son's life, packed him off to Lausanne to complete his studies and reconsider his religious views under the care of the Protestant pastor, Pavillard.

Gibbon stayed in Switzerland for nearly five years and there he laid the solid foundations of his education. His conversion had not gone deep; at Christmas 1754 he was reconciled to the Protestant religion. During the ensuing year he perfected himself in Latin and French, and formed the habit of writing his copious diaries entirely in French. He read French and Latin historians, began to learn Greek, toured Switzerland and wrote for practice ' a very ample relation of my tour '. But his most valuable discovery was the important work on logic of the Abbé de Crousaz, which, he records ' formed my mind to a habit of thinking and reasoning I had no idea of before '. He now began to exercise his critical faculties by writing essays or, as he preferred to call them, ' observations ' on Plautus and Virgil. He corresponded with neighbouring *savants*, saw the plays of Voltaire, and began to compose, in French, his *Essai sur l'Étude de la Littérature*. He knew that he wanted to be a man of learning and a writer, but he aimed at criticism or philosophy rather than history.

In June 1757 he met Suzanne Curchod, a pretty, intelligent, well-read young woman, the only child of a neighbouring pastor. Suzanne had no fortune except her intellect and her charms but she was greatly sought after. Gibbon's entry in his diary is short and telling:

" I saw Mademoiselle Curchod: Omnia vincit amor, et nos cedamus amori."

Gibbon himself was by no means unattractive. Although he was very small, his fresh colour and lively expression gave him charm and his conversation was fluent, witty and erudite; also he appeared to be a young man with a future. Mademoiselle Curchod, who had a good many admirers, was disposed to be coy. Gibbon pursued her. She held him off a little too long and by the time she decided to relent his own ardour was evidently cooling. But he could hardly admit that he had changed his mind, and when he left Switzerland in the spring of 1758, it was on the understanding that he would return to marry her. In his autobiography he gives a laconic and slightly disingenuous account of what next occurred. His father opposed the marriage and Gibbon, in his famous phrase, ' sighed as a lover but obeyed as a son '. He does not explain why, although he came home in May, he did not mention Suzanne to his father until August, nor does he tell of Suzanne's desperate letters, imploring him to be true to her.

Gibbon was not made for domestic life and he probably knew it. He had the egoism of the natural scholar and wrote of himself ' I was never less alone than when by myself '. This is not the temperament that makes an ardent lover or a good husband. In a moment of youthful impulse he had thought himself in love with an intelligent young woman, but it is clear that his love evaporated when he began to think about the responsibilities and commitments of marriage. The sigh that he heaved as a lover was a sigh of relief.

If Gibbon had the egoism very natural to scholars he had also an affectionate and grateful nature and his treatment of Suzanne is the only example of blameable personal conduct in his life. He was a good son although he had some cause for complaint of a father who never did much for him except squander his patrimony. The elder Mr. Gibbon had married again while his son was abroad; and it is much to Gibbon's credit that, although naturally apprehensive at first, he soon became devoted to his step-mother and remained so to the end of his life. In all the ordinary exchanges of family and friendship Gibbon was kind, reasonable, well-behaved and warm-hearted. But when it came to the stronger passions he failed, as scholars commonly do. Those whose first passion is knowledge justly fear the intrusion of any rival interest.

## II

Gibbon was now twenty-one years old. He spoke and wrote French as fluently—at this time more fluently—than he did English. He had fully determined to devote his life to scholarship and writing though he had not yet settled on a subject. But for the next few years family interests and patriotic duty kept him in England. He had seen little of his father as a boy and nothing at all since he left Oxford. An excellent relationship now sprang up between the two, for the older Mr. Gibbon admired his son's erudition and enjoyed his company, and Hester Gibbon, the step-mother, who had no children of her own, was blessedly free from jealousy. In 1761 both father and son volunteered for the Hampshire militia. The Seven Years War was in progress and there were rumours of a possible French invasion. Nothing of the kind happened but Edward Gibbon spent the best part of two years marching about with the troops in Hampshire, living sometimes in billets and sometimes under canvas. Of this period he was later to say that 'the Captain of Hampshire grenadiers . . . has not been useless to the historian of the Roman Empire'. The part played by an English gentleman in local manœuvres hardly seems on a level with the exploits of the great Roman generals and the ferocious barbarian leaders which Gibbon was later to describe. But the good historian should be able to use his own experience to illuminate that of others, and however absurd the comparison between eighteenth-century Hampshire and the battlefields of the fifth century must appear, however wide the difference between Captain Edward Gibbon of the militia and the thundering chiefs of the gothic hordes, there are certain unchanging elements in the soldier's experience which Gibbon learnt to appreciate.

He found much of the life very boring but he was young and strong enough to enjoy, in limited quantities, the rowdier amusements of his fellow officers. He did not however neglect his studies, went on steadily with his reading in all his leisure hours and completed the *Essai sur l'Étude de la Littérature* that he had begun at Lausanne. His proud father persuaded him to have this little work printed and when the King's brother, the Duke of York, came down to inspect the militia Captain Edward Gibbon, again to satisfy his father's whim, presented him with a copy. The Duke, sitting at breakfast in his tent, promised with conventional courtesy to read it as soon as he had time.

The little book is composed in correct but uninspired French, imitated from Montesquieu. Gibbon himself, looking back on it from the eminence of his maturity, found it ' marred by a kind of obscurity and abruptness', confused and badly put together. It is indeed difficult to make out exactly what thesis Gibbon was trying to prove. 'A number of remarks and examples, historical, critical, philosophical, are heaped on each other without method or connection,' said Gibbon disparagingly, and the description is accurate. But the book contains one or two pages which reveal the writer's intelligence and his gift for history. In an admirable passage he compares Tacitus with Livy and praises the former as the ideal of the historian-philosopher. In another, he considers the nature of historical evidence and

the framework of historical cause and effect within which all
the other sciences are contained.

Irksome duty in the militia ended, with the war, in 1763 and
Gibbon, now twenty-six years of age, set out on a second visit
to the continent of Europe. He passed through Paris whence he
wrote home that he had enjoyed better company and conversation in a fortnight than eighteen months in London could supply.
Early in 1764 he was again in Lausanne and was certainly taken
aback when he encountered Suzanne Curchod during an entertainment at Voltaire's house. The unhappy business ended not
too graciously. The poor girl, who was now an orphan and
very poor, still hoped to marry him. She wrote him long
letters, carefully and intelligently criticizing his *Essai sur l'Étude
de la Littérature.* This was not perhaps the wisest way to win
back a lover's heart but even had she used more feminine wiles,
she would not have succeeded. Gibbon was determined to
escape her and, covering the shabbiness of his own conduct by
an easy self-deception, he convinced himself that she was a
shallow and calculating flirt. 'Fille dangereuse et artificielle,'
he wrote censoriously in his diary. Suzanne implored Jean
Jacques Rousseau, then at Geneva, to see Gibbon and reason
with him, but Rousseau replied that he liked nothing he had
heard of Mr. Gibbon and thought him unworthy of her love.
Suzanne gave up hope and shortly after married the elderly
banker Necker.

She had done very well for herself and soon she was inviting
Gibbon to her house to prove to him that she no longer loved
him and that she had made a better match. The procedure was
natural; it was also, as Gibbon did not fail to note in his diary,
rather vulgar. But time smoothed away all asperities. In later
years these uneasy lovers enjoyed a pleasant middle-aged
friendship, and the elderly distinguished historian was once,

to his amusement, the object of a proposal of marriage from Suzanne's precocious little daughter, the future Madame de Stael.

Gibbon was by no means exclusively occupied with Suzanne during his second visit to Lausanne. He renewed his friendship with the Swiss scholar, Deyverdun, who had been tutor to several distinguished young Englishmen including Lord Chesterfield's heir, and he made the acquaintance of another travelling compatriot, John Holroyd, later Lord Sheffield; these two were to be his closest friends for many years. Meanwhile he went on with his studies and accumulated voluminous notes on the ancient monuments of Italy in preparation for his journey there in a few months' time.

He was by now fairly sure that he intended to write history but his mind still wavered between a number of topics. He had considered a history of the Third Crusade, or of the Renaissance wars of France and Italy; or a life of Sir Walter Raleigh; or of the Marquis of Montrose; but by the summer of 1764 the principal subjects had reduced themselves to two: the Fall of the Roman Empire, or the Rise of the Swiss Republic.

About this time he visited the Court of Savoy, an occasion of which he has left a characteristically vivid description. He got on so well with the princesses of Savoy and ' grew so very free and easy that I drew out my snuff box, rapped it, took snuff twice (a crime never known before in the presence chamber) and continued my discourse in my usual attitude of my body bent forward and my forefinger stretched out '. Gibbon was a young man of twenty-seven, with only an obscure pamphlet to his name, but he already had the confidence and the tricks of speech and gesture of a much older and more established scholar. What made Gibbon different from other conceited young men was that he had something more than wide reading and a lively talent for conversation; he had genius, as almost everyone was able to see.

There was another difference. In spite of his assurance, in spite of the vanity which sometimes made him ridiculous, Gibbon had the inner humility of the scholar in the face of his material. He was more eager to learn than to teach.

In the autumn of 1764 he left Lausanne for Italy and by October had reached Rome, whence he wrote, in what for Gibbon is almost a bemused strain, to his step-mother:

> "I have already found such a fund of entertainment for a mind somewhat prepared for it by an acquaintance with the Romans, that I am really almost in a dream. Whatever ideas books may have given us of the greatness of that people, their accounts of the most flourishing state of Rome fall infinitely short of the picture of its ruins . . . I was this morning upon the top of Trajan's pillar. I shall not attempt a description of it. Only figure to yourself a column of a hundred and forty feet high of the purest white marble . . . wrought into bas reliefs with as much taste and delicacy as any chimney piece at Up Park."

The great conception already half formed in Gibbon's mind was taking shape, but he was able—and that is one of the attractive things about Gibbon—to remember that he was writing to a lady with no conception at all of what he was trying to describe; he brings it within the scope of her imagination, in the most natural way in the world, by comparing it to the carved chimney-pieces in a house she often visited.

Gibbon had thoroughly prepared himself for his visit to Rome by making careful notes of the topography of the classical city and the geography of Italy, and by mastering the science of medals which is of paramount importance in the study of Roman history.

The crucial hour was now at hand and he recorded it with due solemnity:

> "It was at Rome, on the 15th of October, 1764, as I sat musing amidst the ruins of the Capitol, while the bare-footed friars were singing vespers in the Temple of Jupiter, that the idea of writing the decline and fall of the city first started to my mind."

Gibbon slightly dramatizes this great moment and it has been pointed out that his diaries show that the idea of writing something on the fall of Rome had been in his thoughts for some months before. But there is a considerable difference between the first foreshadowings of an idea and the moment at which a book takes shape and quickens within the author's mind. It is that moment which Gibbon, with his natural sense of the dramatic, has fixed and recorded.

But other interests still competed with the *Decline and Fall* and on his return to England in 1765 he turned once again from the vices of the Roman Empire to the virtues of the Swiss republic. He composed a long introductory section to a history of Switzerland, in French, and read it aloud to a literary society. By a rare stroke of good fortune, his listeners unanimously condemned it. 'The momentary sensation', writes Gibbon, ' was painful; but their condemnation was ratified by my cooler thoughts. I delivered my imperfect sheets to the flames and for ever after renounced a design in which some expense, much labour and more time had been so vainly consumed.' He had another reason for changing his mind. He did not know German and, although his friend Deyverdun was generously willing to help in this part of the research, he saw that to study the growth of the Swiss Confederation some personal knowledge of this 'barbarous gothic dialect' would be essential. About the same time, fortunately, he was persuaded to drop the curious vanity of writing in French.

So at last, about his thirtieth year, the stage was set for him to begin on his great book. He did not devote himself to it entirely but, in the intervals of his study, lived the easy social life of a cultivated gentleman, dining and conversing among the distinguished men of his time. He was for twelve years an almost entirely silent Member of Parliament and he held a minor government post as a Commissioner of Trade and Plantations, from which he derived a small additional income. This was welcome to him because his father. who had died in 1770, had not left him rich.

### III

The first volume of the *Decline and Fall* appeared in 1776. It carried the story of the Roman Empire from the ordered tranquillity of the Antonine epoch through the intrigues, revolutions and disasters of the third century to the rehabilitation of the Empire under Diocletian and the establishment of Christianity as the official religion under Constantine: a hundred and fifty years of rapidly succeeding events and changing ideas. The opening paragraph of the great book immediately awakens interest, creates a remarkable and comprehensive picture of the age described, and reveals that air of learned and untroubled candour, and that sure and shapely style which was to be maintained throughout the whole gigantic undertaking:

" In the second century of the Christian era, the Empire of

Rome comprehended the fairest part of the earth, and the most civilized portion of mankind. The frontiers of that extensive monarchy were guarded by ancient renown and disciplined valour. The gentle but powerful influence of laws and manners had gradually cemented the union of the provinces. Their peaceful inhabitants enjoyed and abused the advantage of wealth and luxury. The image of a free constitution was preserved with decent reverence: the Roman Senate appeared to possess the sovereign authority, and devolved on the emperors all the executive powers of government. During a happy period (A.D. 98-180) of more than fourscore years, the public administration was conducted by the virtue and abilities of Nerva, Trajan, Hadrian, and the two Antonines. It is the design of this, and of the two succeeding chapters, to describe the prosperous condition of their empire; and afterwards from the death of Marcus Antoninus, to deduce the most important circumstances of its decline and fall; a revolution which will ever be remembered, and is still felt by the nations of the earth."

Horace Walpole, prostrated by an attack of gout in the week of publication, sent round a note congratulating Gibbon on 'the style, manner, method, clearness, and intelligence' of his first chapter and added, ' Mr. Walpole's impatience to proceed will give him such spirits that he flatters himself he shall owe part of his recovery to Mr. Gibbon '. A few days later he was writing to a friend:

"Lo, there is just appeared a truly classic work . . . The style is as smooth as a Flemish picture, and the muscles are concealed and only for natural uses, not exaggerated like Michaelangelo's to show the painter's skill in anatomy. The book is Mr. Gibbon's *Decline and Fall of the Roman Empire*

. . . I know him a little, never suspected the extent of his talents for he is perfectly modest but I intend to know him a great deal more . . ."

Walpole was wrong in imagining Gibbon to be modest, as he was later to discover. In every other respect his judgment has been fully confirmed by time.

The enthusiasm with which literary London received the book was not shared by the Anglican clergy. The first volume contained the famous Chapters XV and XVI devoted to the rise of Christianity and the treatment of Christians by the Roman Empire up to the time of Constantine the Great. Gibbon was not a militant anti-Christian; but he had acquired most of his philosophic ideas in the French-speaking part of Europe, and had come to accept the easy cynicism of contemporary French intellectuals as though it were universal. Their way of thought appealed naturally to his exact, unemotional mind. When he described his subject as ' the triumph of barbarism and Christianity ', when in his autobiography he slyly drew attention to the same thing in concrete form with his striking picture of the ruins of the Capitol and the barefooted friars singing in the Temple of Jupiter, Gibbon was neither throwing out a challenge nor making propaganda against religion; he was stating what he felt to be the only accurate view of the matter. As the Church had gained in power, so Roman civilization had declined: that was the inescapable fact.

The violent attacks which were soon made on his treatment of Christianity astonished and distressed him. ' I was startled ', he writes, ' at the first discharge of ecclesiastical ordnance,' and well he might be for not only were angry pamphlets written against him but he was twice made the object of special attack in a sermon. Most of the criticism was as trivial as it was passionate, but one cleric, the youthful Dr. Davis of Balliol College, Oxford, accused him of misquoting his sources and plagiarizing other writers. These accusations Gibbon answered in a manner that exposed the presumption of his attacker. Gibbon was a thorough and careful scholar and he had a deep and comprehensive knowledge of the available material. It is one of the minor ironies of history that he quarried so much of his book from the source materials laboriously assembled in the previous century by the great antiquarian and scholar Tillemont, himself a devout believer, who, in his pertinacious gathering of the documents, had certainly never intended them to serve the purposes of a writer with so different an outlook on the Church.

Gibbon's treatment of Christianity is in truth more offensive in manner than matter. Sainte-Beuve, whose analysis of Gibbon in *Causeries du Lundi* is particularly illuminating on this question, describes his writing as impregnated with a secret contempt for any feelings that he himself did not share. This contempt is all the more deadly for being cloaked in the guise of urbanity; as, for instance, in the famous paragraph in which he subtly discredits the initial miracles of Christianity.

" But how shall we excuse the supine inattention of the Pagan and philosophic world to those evidences which were presented by the hand of Omnipotence, not to their reason but to their senses? During the age of Christ, of his Apostles, and of their first disciples, the doctrine which they preached was confirmed by innumerable prodigies. The lame walked, the blind saw, the sick were healed, the dead were raised, daemons were expelled, and the laws of nature were frequently suspended for the benefit of the Church. But the sages of Greece and Rome turned aside from the awful spectacle, and, pursuing the ordinary occupations of life and study, appeared unconscious of any alterations in the moral or physical government of the world. Under the reign of Tiberius, the whole earth, or at least a celebrated province of the Roman Empire, was involved in a preternatural darkness of three hours. Even this miraculous event, which ought to have excited the wonder, the curiosity and the devotion of mankind, passed without notice in an age of science and history."

This attitude of ironical superiority towards believers still has the power to exasperate and provoke the devout. But Gibbon was not so much an anti-Christian as an agnostic. It was not religion that he disliked but exaggerated legends or meaningless rituals designed to captivate the multitude or make them amenable to the priest. Significant of this is his famous dictum: ' The various modes of worship which prevailed in the Roman world were all considered by the people equally true, by the philosopher, equally false, and by the magistrates, as equally useful.' This exact and careful statement, relating to a particular epoch, is frequently misquoted, and Gibbon is popularly credited with having said that ' All religions seem to the people equally true, to the philosopher equally false and to the magistrate equally useful '. Whether or not Gibbon would have agreed to so general an assertion, he did not make it. He was too good a historian to generalize widely or wildly and his comments were usually in strict relation to the epoch of which he was writing.

None the less his inability or unwillingness to sympathize with an attitude of mind not his own is a blemish in his great work. It closed his understanding to the irrational forces which can inspire men to wisdom as well as folly. As the fourth century, which principally occupies his first and second volumes, was one of the most deeply and vehemently religious epochs of European history, his blindness on this point can be as irritating to the student of history as it is offensive to the Christian.

The failing is part of Gibbon's character and outlook, that very character and outlook which give to the whole history its air of classic mastery. To wish Gibbon different is to wish the masterpiece unmade, and even while we regret the cynical pleasure which Gibbon evidently felt in demolishing the miracles and reducing the sufferings and the numbers of the Christian martyrs in the Diocletianic persecution we cannot but take pleasure in the sobriety of his argument and the poise of his style:

> " After the church had triumphed over all her enemies, the interest as well as the vanity of the captives prompted them to magnify the merit of their respective suffering. A convenient distance of time or place gave an ample scope to the progress of fiction; and the frequent instances which might be alleged of holy martyrs whose wounds had been instantly healed, whose strength had been renewed, and whose lost members had been miraculously restored, were extremely convenient for the purpose of removing every difficulty, and of silencing every objection. The most extravagant legends, as they conduced to the honour of the church, were applauded by the credulous multitude, countenanced by the power of the clergy, and attested by the suspicious evidence of ecclesiastical history."

Gibbon goes on to investigate the statistics of the glorious army of the martyrs and to suggest that, after all, only a small number ' sacrificed their lives for the important purpose of introducing Christianity into the world '.

The arguments in this passage are unexceptionable. But the tone implies not only an unwillingness to accept false martyrs and invented sacrifices but a disparagement of the emotions which inspired genuine martyrs to make real sacrifices.

This weakness in the book is also its greatness. It is Gibbon's capacity for writing of passionate and desperate times with a cool mind that enables him to write in general with such untroubled objectivity. It was not his gift to understand the hearts of men, but it was his duty and pleasure to understand their minds. He took great pains not only to read essential contemporary sources, but to be fully acquainted with the literature and the other productions of the ages he studied. If he did not understand the heart of a Christian slave he understood the mind of a Roman senator. If he did not greatly value the human passions he set the highest possible value on the human intellect. His own mind had developed in the favourable atmosphere of a time which delighted to call itself the Age of Reason. As one of his most acute modern critics, Mr. Christopher Dawson, has said, ' he stood on the summit of the Renaissance achievement, and looked back over the waste of history to ancient Rome, as from one mountain top to another. The tragedy for him is the dethronement of a noble and intelligent civilization by force and ignorance. It is the triumph of the illiterate and the irrational that he records and deplores '.

While he understood the minds and the calculations of the people about whom he wrote, he did not, like the romantic historians, throw himself into their hearts and try to share their feelings. The historic present—Carlyle's favourite tense—is practically unknown to Gibbonian grammar, a point of language which strikingly illustrates the change which the romantic movement wrought in the treatment of history.

But if Gibbon is not conventionally religious, neither is he indifferent to moral standards. He assumes that it is the right and duty of the historian to have a clearly defined moral attitude and he is exquisitely skilful in introducing judgment by way of implication. With what quiet contempt he deals for instance with the barbarian Ricimer, who, in the fifth century, elevated and destroyed puppet emperors at will. One of these, Majorian, was not only a man of strong and noble character but an old companion in arms. Majorian strove to revive the ancient discipline of the Romans; this did not suit Ricimer and he had to go. ' It was not perhaps without some regret ', writes Gibbon, ' that Ricimer sacrificed his friend to the interest of his ambition.' In fifteen words he more perfectly exposes the baseness of Ricimer than he could have done in a paragraph of rhetoric. He carries on the story in the same tone:

> " He resolved in a second choice to avoid the imprudent preference of superior virtue and merit. At his command the obsequious senate of Rome bestowed the Imperial title on Libius Severus, who ascended the throne of the West without emerging from the obscurity of a private condition. History has scarcely deigned to notice his birth, his elevation, his character or his death. Severus expired as soon as his life became inconvenient to his patron."

Gibbon's just and generous admiration is reserved for those who best display the classic virtues; justice, fortitude, perseverance, moderation. He greatly admires cleverness but never for itself alone. His morality, classical again in this, did not permit him to respect success unless it was allied with the virtues. He admires Diocletian, the hard-working self-made man who restored order to a distracted Empire more than Constantine who succeeded to his work and whose sly calculations and mercenary attitude to religion he found contemptible. He

admires the men who failed nobly, like Julian the Apostate, or
Majorian who strove to save the tottering fabric, and he despises
those who succeeded ignobly.


## IV


Gibbon's reputation was established by the publication of his
first volume which ends with the triumph of Constantine. He
was now something more than an erudite man and a good
*raconteur*. He was an established historian equal in fame to Hume
and Robertson, the two great figures whom he had admired in
his youth. His vanity grew with his fame, or at least became
more apparent, but since his achievement justified it and he had
with it so much genuine good humour, his friends were disposed
to regard it as an engaging foible. When he told an anecdote
or illustrated an argument he liked to be listened to, and the
gesture he has himself so well described—the body bent forward
and the forefinger extended—was designed to attract the attention that it commanded. But he was not a conversation killer;
he knew how to take part in a general discussion; and one of
his younger friends, Lord Sheffield's daughter, was to leave it
on record that he had a great gift for drawing out the opinions
anp ideas of the young people he met. This capacity argues a
genuine interest in the ideas of others and a benevolence which
counteracted the effects of his vanity.

But he did not like to be put out of countenance. Once at a
dinner party he had told a good story and ' with his customary
tap on the lid of his snuff box was looking round to receive our
tribute of applause, when a deep-toned but clear voice was heard
from the bottom of the table very calmly and civilly impugning
the correctness of the narrative '. Gibbon defended his position,

but the deep-toned clear voice, which was that of the youngest guest present, would not be silenced. Seeing defeat imminent, Gibbon hurried from the table and was found by his host looking for his hat and cloak. 'That young gentleman', said Gibbon, 'is, I have no doubt, extremely ingenious and agreeable but I must acknowledge that his style of conversation is not exactly what I am accustomed to, so you must positively excuse me.'

The young gentleman, twenty-one at the time, was William Pitt, who would be Chancellor of the Exchequer at twenty-three, and Prime Minister at twenty-four. In later life he came to value Gibbon's company as Gibbon did his. Gibbon's vanity made him like the sensitive plant; he wilted for a moment at an aggressive touch but he soon recovered and retained no malice.

In 1779, four years after the publication of his first volume, Gibbon brought out the second volume, devoted to the invasions of the barbarians and the Circus quarrels at Constantinople. The subject was not so much to the liking of the polite society of the eighteenth century as that of the earlier volume, and Horace Walpole, who had so deeply admired the first, was disposed to be critical, objecting that so much time and skill should be spent on so unrewarding a theme. Gibbon was highly offended. He seems to have taken with much more humour the reception he got from the King's brother, the Duke of Gloucester, to whom he presented a copy. 'Another damned thick book?' exclaimed the affable prince. 'Always scribble, scribble, scribble, eh, Mr. Gibbon?'

With the fall of Lord North's government Gibbon lost the small post on which he had depended for part of his income. He decided therefore that he would be able to live more peacefully and more cheaply in Lausanne, and by the autumn of 1783 he transferred himself and his library to a delightful house which

126

he planned to share with his old friend Deyverdun. The two scholars occupied separate parts of their pleasant mansion but met for dinner over which they discussed the problems and pleasures of their work, and entertained their friends from time to time. Lausanne society still abounded, as it had in Gibbon's youth, with intelligent and well-behaved ladies, and the two middle-aged scholars sometimes wistfully thought that a wife between them would not come amiss. 'Deyverdun and I have often agreed in jest and in earnest that a house like ours would be regulated, graced and enlivened by an agreeable female companion, but each of us seems desirous that his friend should sacrifice himself for the public good.' Each of them feared the obligations more than he valued the advantages of taking so momentous a step and they continued their bachelor existence. Gibbon knew how fortunate he was and wrote with a full sense of his blessings to Lady Sheffield describing his new library which commanded from ' three windows of plate glass, an unbounded prospect of many a league of vineyard, of fields, of wood, of lake and of mountains '. He concluded with satisfaction: ' An excellent house, a good table, a pleasant garden, are no contemptible ingredients in human happiness.'

Gibbon's common sense is one of his most attractive qualities. He did not want more than he had from life, and certainly he had everything that a scholar could want. But comfortable means and ample leisure do not content everyone and many writers have been as happily circumstanced as Gibbon without being so contentedly aware of the fact or so grateful for their blessings. Gibbon was firmly and rightly contemptuous of the delusion, shared by many eighteenth-century intellectuals, that the ignorant peasant, free from the anxieties and speculations of the educated and powerful, was much to be envied. Frederick the Great was reported to have said to d'Alembert, as they walked in the garden of Sans Souci, that a poor old woman, whom they saw asleep on a sunny bank was happier than they. 'The King and the philosopher may speak for themselves,' wrote Gibbon, 'for my part I do not envy the old woman.'

It was Gibbon's pleasant habit to work in a small pavilion at the end of his garden and here he finished the last volume of his great work, a moment commemorated in a famous passage in his autobiography. 'It was on the day, or rather the night, of the 27th June 1787, between the hours of eleven and twelve that I wrote the last lines of the last page in a summer-house in my garden. After laying down my pen I took several turns in a *berceau* or covered walk of Acacias, which commands a prospect of the country, the lake, and the mountains. The air was temperate, the sky was serene, the silver orb of the moon was reflected from the waters, and all Nature was silent. I will not dissemble the first emotions of joy on the recovery of freedom, and perhaps the establishment of my fame. But my pride was soon humbled, and a sober melancholy was spread over my mind by the idea that I had taken my everlasting leave of an old and agreeable companion, and that whatsoever might be the future fate of my history, the life of the historian must be short and precarious.'

The quietude and peace of that scene is illuminating. Gibbon was a great writer, and his book meant everything to him, but he never seems to have had—indeed it is unthinkable that he should have had—that intense relationship for love, hate, and exasperation that many great writers have with their work. His attitude to it is well behaved and under control like his writing: 'an old agreeable companion'.

The *Decline and Fall* itself ends with a deliberately low-toned passage. Sainte-Beuve, with his usual perspicacity, has said that Gibbon finishes 'cette longue carrière comme une promenade', and at the moment of setting down his pen pauses to consider the view and to take his ease. The closing paragraph describes the gradual unearthing of imperial Rome from the rubble of the Middle Ages. There is just a suggestion, but only a suggestion, of the new dawn, after the six volumes which have discussed the long decay and the final collapse of anything resembling or carrying on the tradition of the Roman Empire:

" Prostrate obelisks were raised from the ground, and erected in the most conspicuous places; of the eleven aqueducts of the Cæsars and consuls, three were restored; the artificial rivers were conducted over a long series of old, or of new, arches, to discharge into marble basins a flood of salubrious and refreshing waters; and the spectator, impatient to ascend the steps of St. Peter's, is detained by a column of Egyptian granite, which rises between two lofty and perpetual fountains, to the height of one hundred and twenty feet. The map, the description, the monuments of ancient Rome, have been elucidated by the diligence of the antiquarian and the student; and the footsteps of heroes, the relics not of superstition, but of empire, are devoutly visited by a new race of pilgrims from the remote, and once savage, countries of the North."

That is the end of the book proper. Gibbon added a postscript, and after twenty years of work he could hardly have done less: he briefly summed up the story that he had tried to tell and concluded: ' It was among the ruins of the Capitol that I first conceived the idea of a work which has amused and exercised twenty years of my life, and which however inadequate to my own wishes I finally deliver to the curiosity and candour of the public.' To anyone acquainted with the sufferings and struggles of the writer, the exhilarations and frustrations and fallacious triumphs, or with the labours and problems of historical research, that phrase 'amused and exercised' must seem what perhaps it is—an understatement. Yet it may not be. The judicious use of exact but unexaggerated terms produces exact and unexaggerated reactions. Gibbon's style reflects and may also partly have shaped his character.

He came to England for the publication of his last three volumes, was given a splendid dinner by his publisher, attended the trial of Warren Hastings, and was made the object of a delicate compliment from Sheridan in his speech for the prosecution. 'Nothing equal in criminality is to be found', said Sheridan, 'either in ancient or modern history, in the correct periods of Tacitus or the luminous pages of Gibbon . . .' Later he teased Gibbon by asserting that he had said not 'luminous', but 'voluminous'.


## V


It was now 1788, a year before the fall of the Bastille. The political storms in which the century was to end were about to break and literary fashions were moving fast away from the detached manner of Gibbon towards the subjective and emotional manner of the romantics. In this year—1788—Schiller's play *Don Carlos* appeared as well as his passionate and vivid history of the Revolt of the Netherlands; Goethe's *Egmont* is of the same year. The turbulent reaction from the logic and order of French thought towards the exaltation of the passions and the ideal of a wild liberty was well on the way. Mirabeau, who had come to England shortly before the Revolution in search of radical inspiration in a country whose liberal institutions had been praised by Voltaire, looked about for English historians to translate into French. For Gibbon, the greatest of them all, he felt only disapproval. At a large dinner party he fixed an indignant stare on a fat little man who had been pointed out to him as the author of the *Decline and Fall*, and spent the meal rehearsing what he would say to him. ' You, an Englishman! ' he would say. ' No, you cannot be. You, who admire an empire of more than two hundred millions of men not one of whom could call himself free. You who extol an effeminate philosophy which sets greater value on luxury and pleasures than on virtue; you who write in a style which is always elegant but never vigorous —you are not an Englishman but at most a slave of the Elector of Hanover.' His courage, perhaps fortunately, failed him, for the object of his angry glaring was guiltless of the *Decline and Fall*. Gibbon was in Lausanne at the time.

Mirabeau's view is unfair; like many other critics of Gibbon, he had not read the book. What Gibbon admired in the Roman Empire was not its expanse and power, still less its authority over the individual. What he admired was the spectacle of peaceful order which enabled the arts of civilization to be practised. He did not admire effeminate philosophies and luxuries, and he deplored the decay of democratic institutions while appreciating the craft with which successive Emperors had curtailed them. His admiration was reserved for the strong classical virtues, for reason and restraint.

If the reformers and revolutionaries, and the poor young *exaltés* of liberty who were soon to have such a rude awakening, found much to criticize in Gibbon's book its reception among the discriminating older generation surpassed even the author's by no means modest hopes. Adam Smith pronounced him ' at the very head of the whole literary tribe at present existing in Europe '. He was generally acclaimed as the greatest of English historians—a position from which he has not yet been dethroned.

131

On his return to Lausanne after his triumph in London he found things were no longer what they had been. His friend Deyverdun was dead. The romantic movement had launched upon the country a quantity of staring tourists, come ' to view the glaciers '. Gibbon was also perturbed by the ' furious spirit of democracy ' which had been let loose by the French Revolution. His own political views are best summed up in the comment which he made at this time on the internal politics of Switzerland. Lausanne, long unwillingly subjected to the aristocratic government of Berne, was stirring uneasily. Gibbon had no patience with this nonsense: ' While the aristocracy of Berne protects the happiness, it is superfluous to enquire whether it be founded on the rights, of man,' he wrote.

Fascinated by the politics of the past, he was resentful of the politics of the present because they threatened his calm retreat. Lausanne was now full of refugees from the Revolution. ' These noble fugitives ', he wrote, ' are entitled to our pity; they claim our esteem, but they cannot, in their present state of mind and fortune, much contribute to our amusement. Instead of looking down as calm and idle spectators on the theatre of Europe, our domestic harmony is somewhat embittered by the infusion of party spirit.' The comment is curiously insensitive, and Gibbon's public comments are indeed often out of key with the natural kindliness he showed in his personal life.

In the summer of 1793 his great friend Lord Sheffield was suddenly left a widower. His wife, reacting very differently from Gibbon, had fallen ill owing to long and strenuous hours of work on behalf of homeless French refugees in England. Gibbon, genuinely distressed at his friend's grief, hurried home to console him. He passed the summer between London and Lord Sheffield's country house and was able both to give comfort and to receive much pleasure from the company of Lord

Sheffield's daughters and their young friends. He was only fifty-six and at the height of his intellectual power. A great edition of English mediæval documents, of which he was to be the editor, was projected and he looked forward to the new work, declaring with confidence that he was good for ten or twelve more years of valuable work. But his friends had grown alarmed for the state of his health. His vanity prevented him from admitting that the hydrocele from which he was suffering had reached embarrassingly large proportions. At length, however, he agreed to an operation in the autumn of 1793. This was temporarily successful but the condition worsened again in January. Gibbon was now taking quinine every six hours and drinking five glasses of Madeira at dinner on doctor's orders. In the circumstances it is not surprising that the immediate cause of his death, on 17th January 1794, appears to have been cirrhosis of the liver.

English history lost a remarkable piece of editing when Gibbon died before he could begin work on the documents. But anything after the *Decline and Fall* would have been an anticlimax. His life's work is the one massive, incomparable book, and all the rest that he left behind him is interesting chiefly for the light it throws on the mind and the method behind the great history.

The *Decline and Fall* stands alone in English historical literature. Style and structure apart, its erudition still amazes; what other history has stood the test of seven generations of scholarship and criticism without being wholly superseded? Gibbon's views have been modified and added to; yet his book remains basically a standard work for the decline of Rome, at least, if not for the Byzantine empire.

Of the style and structure it is hard to speak briefly. His unique quality—unique, that is, among English narrative historians—is his exact control. Most English historians of any literary sensibility are given to passion; the quality is inherent in the calling. They become involved in the events they describe, are moved, excited, carried away. This makes for powerful writing and sometimes for a sharper insight into character, but it does not make for a steady, comprehensive vision, or for clear presentation.

The English as writers have a false conception of themselves. We do not think of ourselves as passionate, yet the great strength and almost all the faults of English writing arise from passion. We are among the most passionate and impulsive writers in the modern world. We commonly set more value on something called ' sincerity '—a word which often describes what happens when a writer loses control of his material—than on symmetry and order. We are the first to condemn a deliberate and perfected work of art as ' dead '. Sometimes this judgment may be right, but often it is no more than an angry prejudice arising from our own vehement and untidy minds. Consider for instance how few Englishmen are really capable of appreciating the flawless achievement of Racine. Shakespeare, the transcendent artist who broke all the rules, had left to his countrymen an unwritten charter to despise them.

Gibbon was not entirely without passion, for his love of learning and reverence for the intellect amounted to passion. But he kept it within bounds and when he wrote, his first thought was for the whole work of art. Each sentence performs its right function in relation to what goes before and after, each paragraph carries the narrative on at the necessary pace, or establishes a point in the exposition. Because of this attention to detail the massive volumes are always easy to read and never monotonous. The narrative passages are never clogged with too much imagination, and the expository paragraphs and chapters stand out with a fine static clarity. Gibbon's control of his material was so sure and his sense of form so strong that he seems to have been able, at least in his later volumes, to achieve his effects without rewriting. His plan was clear in advance and he would write his sentences in his head and commit them to paper only when he was satisfied of their completeness. In earlier times, when he still rewrote substantially, it seems to have been the form or order of each chapter rather than the shape of each sentence which gave him anxiety. Of his first volume he wrote to Lord Sheffield: ' The first chapter has been composed *de nouveau*, three times, the second twice ' and he spoke of an intention to ' *refondre* ' or recast other important parts of the book.

Gibbon's style is highly cultivated and therefore artificial. It is also a dangerous style to copy and he has suffered badly from imitators who aped his mannerisms without understanding their purpose and without having the sensitive ear and varied vocabulary which made it possible for him to use them with effect. He had, for instance, a trick of pairing words; open the great volumes anywhere and you find phrases like this—' *The relaxation of discipline* and the *disuse of exercise* rendered the soldiers *less able* and *less willing* to support the fatigues of the service.'

This is not done merely to add a spurious weightiness to simple statements. It is done, almost always, with the express purpose of slowing down the narrative at those points on which Gibbon wants the reader's mind to dwell. He thus detains the reader's attention by the simple device of making him read more slowly. But he never exactly duplicates his phrases; the additions are artistically correct, because they add to or modify the meaning. In the hands of less skilful writers, who duplicated without art and without apparent reason, the trick which was widely copied became intolerable.

The chance by which the *Decline and Fall* came to be written looks almost providential; here was an English mind with the romantic bent of the English—evident in his early reading and tastes—carefully cultivated in the French tradition and saturated with French culture. He produced in consequence, in the most exact and expressive English, a history which is a model of lucid exposition and balanced form yet which never loses that undercurrent of feeling essential to great historical writing.

The *Decline and Fall of the Roman Empire* is an outstanding work of English scholarship and one of the great monuments of English eighteenth-century literature. This double achievement has had a profound influence on the whole tradition of English historical writing. The increasing complexity of techniques of historical research, and the ever more exacting standards of scholarly accuracy which began to prevail in the later nineteenth century, thanks to the massive and precise scholarship of the Germans, inevitably divorced history from literature. But in England this divorce never became complete and the re-union of history and literature in this country in our own time, may be traced in part to the influence of Gibbon. His method and manner and his splendid assurance may no longer be the models by which modern English historians work but he remains the presiding genius of our historical literature. The union of knowledge and style which he achieved is still the ideal of the English tradition.

*PART II*

# SEVENTEENTH CENTURY
## SKETCHES

# THE LAST MASQUE

THE DRESS designed for King Charles I to wear in the
masque which concluded the Christmas festivities of the
year 1639-40 was of pale blue embroidered with silver thread.
Inigo Jones, who had designed the sets for every masque for the
last thirty years, had once again revived the fashions of his
youth with their tight-fitting doublets and padded breeches.
For the sleeves he had adapted one of his favourite flower motifs:
calyx-shaped over-sleeves enveloped the King's shoulders and
upper arms, like the inverted cups of gigantic bluebells. The
doublet, closely moulded to his slight figure, was so thickly
stitched over in silver whorls and posies that the blue background
hardly showed. His padded breeches were of slashed blue and
silver, the blue edged with filigree thread. Long white silk
stockings encased his small but well-made legs, exposed up to
the thigh. His dancing pumps were all but concealed under
huge silver shoe-roses. A quilled ruff of fine muslin framed his
face, and his greying hair, carefully curled, was surmounted
by a three-cornered hat of cloth of silver above which nodded
two tiers of well-matched ostrich plumes.

King Charles was mature for masquerading. He was in his
fortieth year and, but for his Master of the Ordnance, Lord
Newport, the oldest performer in that year's festivities. Although
the King had been rehearsing with his usual assiduity since the
previous October, his more serious and distinguished courtiers

had been too deeply engaged in the affairs of the nation to have much time to spare. Apart from the eight lords he had chosen to attend him, the performers were mostly drawn from the pages and musicians, the small fry of Whitehall.

The King's part was suited to his age and dignity. He had only to appear on a throne of honour raised high above the stage and later to partner the Queen in a stately dance. It was the responsibility of Inigo Jones to see that no embarrassing accidents occurred. " The peece of tymber of ye engyne of ye Kings seate to be strongly nayled and fastened " he scribbled on his sketch of the backstage mechanics.

The King's seat on the English throne in January 1640 was less comfortable than the stout wooden contraption designed for him by Inigo Jones. The atmosphere of gaiety which normally surrounded the Christmas celebrations of the Court was notably absent, and although both the King and Queen appeared as enthusiastic about their masque as usual, there was in their conduct a hint of pretence. The iron-handed minister, Wentworth, recently recalled from Ireland and created Earl of Strafford, had been in frequent audience with the King. He was not among the masquers. Both his austere presence and that of the buff-coated officers who now haunted the palace disturbed the jocund mood proper to the season.

The words of the masque had been written by William Davenant, the music composed by the Queen's master musician, Louis Richard, a Frenchman long resident at the English Court. In the opinion of everyone, not least of Inigo Jones himself, words and music were secondary to the scenic inventions for which they provided the vehicle. But a plot and a subject of some kind there had to be. King Charles, therefore, would impersonate the character of Philogenes, the lover of his people, a beneficent ruler conferring the blessings of peace upon a chorus

representing the grateful nation. The King rehearsed the part
in the intervals of the harassing Council meetings at which he
decided to equip an army of thirty thousand foot and three
thousand horse to keep his rebellious subjects in order.

The trouble had begun a year before in Scotland, but showed
signs of spreading southward. In the previous summer, confronted by a superior force of rebel Scots at Berwick, the King
had had to make temporary concessions to the rebels and with-
draw without striking a blow. It had been a harsh forewarning
of difficulties to come. His English troops, raised with difficulty,
had been meagre and mutinous. An odd kind of volunteers, a
wit had said, for not a man of them had come willingly. Mur-
murs against the King's church policy, against prelacy and
popery, were growing loud in every English county. On the
march north against the Scots, Lord Say and Lord Brook had
refused to take the special oath of allegiance tendered by the
King to all his followers, promising " most constantly and
cheerfully even to the uttermost hazard of life and fortune to
assist him against any rebels whatsoever." He had had to place
them under arrest: only for a few days, of course, but it had
been an unseemly and perplexing incident. When Lord Say was
released he went home and took his contingent of troops with
him, announcing that they had come solely as his attendants.

Yet with an obscure tenacity the King rejected the evidence
of his subjects' discontent. This must be something superficial,
temporary. It could not be that he, King Charles, the good,
the just, who referred his every action to God and his conscience, should be wantonly defied merely because he wanted
to impose a beautiful uniformity of worship throughout his
dominions.

After he had made his temporary concessions to the rebel
Scots at Berwick, agreeing to suspend his religious reforms in

their country for the time being, he had reviewed the army which had marched against him. The troops, in innocent enthusiasm, threw up their blue bonnets and cried " God save King Charles and down with the Bishops." He was not pleased: he would compel them to respect his bishops yet. To the Scots lords who waited on him he had been cold. When they made to kiss his hand, he withheld it and only slightly raised his hat in a general salutation before taking his seat. His puzzled eyes travelled over their faces, seeking the private reasons for their public opposition. To his certain knowledge there were only five or six of them to whom, in his own phrase, " he had not done courtesies." In his opinion past courtesies should have secured present loyalty; he could conceive of none but personal motives for rebellion. That these men should seriously, for reasons of conscience or patriotism, object to the liturgy that he had had specially composed for Scotland was beyond his imagination.

When he left Berwick after the pacification he had learned his lesson after his own fashion. In future, he announced, " I shall not command but where I am sure to be obeyed." He would be patient and wily; opponents could be removed, bribed, persuaded. He would call into being again the old animosity between English and Scots; he would raise a larger army. He would compel obedience. He would do everything except abandon the policy which he knew to be pleasing to God.

As he moved southwards to London the warm reception of his English subjects, profoundly relieved that there was to be no war, applied a deceptive balm to his injured spirit.

> *Others by war their conquests gain,*
> *You, like a God, your ends obtain,*

## The Last Masque

*Who, when rude chaos for his help did call,*
*Spoke but the word and sweetly ordered all . .*

The Cambridge poet Cowley told him what he wanted to hear. The pacification at Berwick had been of his choosing; he had not been defeated; he, the merciful King, had decided not to fight.

The theme was taken up and elaborated in the masque for which on the afternoon of Tuesday, January 21st, 1640, the whole Court, with a number of ambassadors and distinguished guests, had assembled in the building behind the banqueting house of Whitehall. For the occasion the cares of state had to be excluded, like the bleak January weather, beyond the world of expensive make-believe which was to be conjured up on the stage of the Queen's Dancing Barn. The name had been rudely given to the new building by the Puritans, but in reality it was the King's Dancing Barn, for it had been his idea. Once they had used the banqueting hall itself for masques, but since the painted canvases of Rubens had been hoisted into place on the ceiling, the King feared the damaging effect of candles and torches on their colours. He had given order for the temporary wooden building alongside and it had been constructed to the designs of Inigo Jones, with a permanent stage measuring fifty-two feet in height and forty-two feet from side to side of the proscenium arch. The stage itself was raised from seven to eight feet above the floor of the room, allowing for the construction and working of substantial mechanism underneath.

The seats and boxes in the auditorium were designed to accommodate spectators according to their rank. The central place this afternoon was filled by the royal children and their grandmother. The children, of whom the eldest was not yet ten, were a handsome, high-spirited group, taking strongly after their mother's family—large features, high colouring, bouncing vitality. Their maternal grandmother, Marie de Medici, the only adult royalty among the audience, since the King and Queen had disappeared into their robing-rooms, commanded the scene. She was a substantial woman in her later sixties, her fat-enveloped face eloquent of character rather than intelligence.

After quarrelling for the last time with her son, the King of France, she had thrown herself embarrassingly on the hospitality of her daughter, the Queen of England, In the delicate state of English public opinion the presence of the extravagant Italian visitor with a large train of priests and servants, made an unfortunate impression. Her manner of living at St. James's Palace, which her son-in-law had assigned to her, emphasized inopportunely his Queen's foreign and Roman Catholic connections.

The masque had been devised with the Queen's mother and the royal children in mind. In deference to Marie de Medici's ignorance of English there was little speaking, and the usual interludes of spoken comedy had been replaced by a series of farcical dances. For the delight of the children the scene changes were to be many and all the incidents short.

While the usual preliminary hitches occurred and were dealt with behind the scenes, the audience had plenty to occupy it in deciphering the meaning of the allegorical figures and symbols painted on the cornice, the proscenium arch and the drop-curtain which concealed the stage. In the centre of this curtain appeared the classical name of the performance they were about to see— *Salmacida Spolia*—and those who understood the allusion could explain to those who did not how certain savage tribes had been subdued by the Greeks of Halicarnassus, not by force of arms, but by visiting the fountain of Salmacis, where they saw and learnt to appreciate the superior civilization of the Greeks. So, it was to be understood, the rebellious Scots would learn to appreciate the superior qualities of episcopal government. On one side of the stage two female figures, representing Reason and Intellectual Appetite, were clasping hands. Opposite them " a grave old man representing Counsel " kept company with an armed woman for Resolution. On the deep cornice which surmounted the stage, figures of women and children with symbolic attributes jostled one another. Here were Fame and Safety, Riches, Forgetfulness of Injuries, Commerce, Felicity, " Affection to the country, holding a grasshopper," Prosperity and Innocence.

Presently an anticipatory hush foretold the rising of the curtain. Fans of matched and curled ostrich feathers ceased their movement and lay still in velvet laps; white explanatory hands dropped into repose; all faces turned the same way and, rustling over its roller at tremendous speed, up went the curtain.

Before them, in the cavern of the stage, was a scene of gloom and tempest. Trees with tormented branches bowed before the gale. In the distance angry waves broke over a rock and a storm-driven ship shuddered under a lightning-riven sky. The rattling of metal sheets in the wings added to the awful effect. In the middle of the stage stood a huge round object, recognizable from the outlines painted upon it as the great globe itself.

The audience had possessed themselves of the horror of the scene when with a clap of thunder the globe split in half and a hideous Fury " looking askance with hollow envious eyes " came snarling to the front of the stage, torch in hand. In a harsh male voice, belying her female draperies, the creature began to speak:

*How am I grieved the world should everywhere*
*Be vexed into a storm, save only here?*
*Thou over happy, too much lucky isle . . .*

In rhymed couplets the monster declared her intention of destroy-
ing the peace of England. Lest the meaning should be still in
doubt, the speaking Fury was joined by three others who emphasized the point in a menacing dance.

This was the opening anti-masque. The first of the scene-
changes followed. The shutters forming the wings slid back
along grooves out of sight, revealing another series of shutters
behind them. The dark clouds which hung down from the top
of the scene were wound up creakingly while others of a
different hue began to appear. The stormy sea at the back of the
stage divided down the middle and slid apart to reveal another
painted scene. Since it was not the fashion for the curtain to
drop during these operations, there had long been arguments
among the producers of masques as to the best way of diverting
the attention of spectators. An Italian producer—and the Italians
were the acknowledged masters of the masque—advised the
placing of stooges far back among the audience to cause a dis-
turbance at the critical moment. The simulated cracking of
wood as though a tier of the gallery were collapsing, or a cry of
" Fire! Murder! Help! " could be guaranteed to draw all
attention away from the stage. But the stooges sometimes acted
too well; there had been panics and whole theatres had been
emptied in a stampede for safety. Inigo Jones preferred his own
invention—a gyrating coronal of three concentric circles of
candles set off by reflectors which, being set in motion when a
scene change was to take place, delighted and dazzled the audience
so that they had eyes for nothing else.

But there is no sign of the use of this invention, or of anything else, among the numerous sketches which were made for the masque of 1640. The scene-changes in this, the most mechanically ambitious of all his masques, were apparently effected with so much rapidity that they needed no concealment. The scenery was wound off at each side and up and down from below and above. Behind the numerous canvas clouds which were suspended from braces in the roof and lowered or raised at will, all manner of rapid modifications could be made in the scenery and furnishings of the top part of the stage. They were wonderful clouds, carefully painted and cut after the numerous loving and lyrical sketches which have survived in his papers, small and large, round and elongated, billowing cumulus clouds carefully copied from nature to serve the higher ingenuities of his art.

Before the eyes of the spectators, therefore, the stormy sea and lowering sky gave place to a landscape of smiling summer. Across the painted sky jerked a painted Zephyr on a cloud breathing a flowery breeze from his fat cheeks. Below stretched a saffron-yellow cornfield, improbably framed in arching elm trees round whose knotted trunks grape-bearing vines were garlanded.

Meanwhile, below the stage strong hands turned the windlass which governed the silver chariot now slowly descending from the clouds. Two persons were unsteadily seated within it— a woman in blue ornamented with bulrushes, and a young man "in a carnation garment embroidered all with flowers." In mid-air the two broke into a duet. The lady, who represented Concord, expressed her reluctance to remain longer among the ungrateful people of Great Britain. Her companion, who was the Good Genius of Great Britain, remonstrated with her. The people might be unappreciative, he admitted, but they had a King whom she must surely find it a pleasure to serve:

147

*Yet stay, oh stay, if but to please*
*The great and wise Philogenes.*

It was true, the couple pursued their argument, that the
people were sullen and ungrateful and would not accept their
monarch's benevolent control; but to reward so good a King,
Concord might yet give his people another chance. The har-
monious lecture on politics at an end, the chariot reached stage-
level and the two heavenly beings climbed out of it and departed
in different directions to see whether their persuasions would
soften the hearts of the ungrateful subjects of Philogenes.

Their endeavours would take time, as some of the better-
informed members of the audience may well, a little grimly,
have been thinking. The passage of time had, however, been
allowed for by Davenant in composing his libretto: after their
departure the remaining anti-masques, a series of twenty separate
comic dances, were to be presented, mostly by the younger
members of the Court, pages and young gentlemen, with their
fortunes to make, who had grasped the opportunity of displaying
their amiable talents before the great. Of this half-hour's frolic
nothing has remained but Davenant's brief descriptive note on
each entry and a few unidentifiable sketches of grotesques by
Inigo Jones. Most of the dances were funny and most of the
jokes were topical: ballets about doctors and prescriptions, about
Rosicrucians and Roaring Boys, Jealous Dutchmen and Mad
Lovers. Occasionally the mind's eye can supply a guess from
the stage direction: " Four Grotesques or drollities in the most
fantastical shapes imaginable "; or, the sentimental interlude, a
shepherd dancing a pastoral *pas seul*; or pure farce, " a nurse
and three children in long coats, with bibs, biggins, and muck-
enders." Then there was the dance specially put in for the
Queen's dwarf, Jeffrey Hudson; "three Swiss, one a little

148

Swiss, who played the wag with them as they slept." Three
feet high and twenty-one years old, Jeffrey Hudson concealed
an alert intelligence in his mouse-coloured head and a valiant
spirit in his breast. His portraits reveal the full-size personality
in the midget figure. A year or two later he would be a captain
of horse and would be knighted, not undeservedly, for courage
in the field.

When he had first been brought to the King, Charles had
already been in possession of two other notable curiosities—his
giant porter, and " Old Parr ", the English Methuselah, said to
be a hundred and fifty years of age, and brought to Court by
the Earl of Arundel. " You have lived much longer than other
men," said the King, when the venerable father was presented
to him; " what have you done that was more remarkable? "
The rustic replied with what had long been his best crack:
" Please your Majesty, I did penance for a bastard when I was
above a hundred years old." King Charles uttered a freezing
reproof; but if he regretted old Parr's morals he valued his
years and used to boast that his kingdom contained the tallest
man, the smallest man, and the oldest man in the world.

But Old Parr's vitality had not survived the pace of life at
Court; both he and the giant porter were long since dead, and
Jeffrey Hudson, capering waggishly upon the prostrate bodies
of his fellow-dancers, was now the sole survivor of the
astounding trio.

The interludes had now lasted for long enough. Concord and
the Genius of Great Britain had assembled the full chorus of the
" Beloved People " of England in the wings. The last ballet, a
rollicking affair of a Spanish riding-master and his pupils, galloped
off the stage. The side shutters rattled once more along their
grooves, the clouds were lowered and raised, and the cornfields
at the back changed to a mountain landscape, in the midst of

which, on a high, hollow mountain, above defiles of rock and pine, the clouds hung mysteriously low. While the scene was changing the chorus had crowded on to the stage and facing the very centre of the audience began to sing a compliment to the Queen Mother. There she sat, the stupid, stout, unloved widow of Henry of Navarre. " Your beauty kept his valour's flame alive," they shamelessly chanted, " Your Tuscan wisdom taught him how to thrive."

Now, at last, the great moment had come. The chorus of the Beloved People ranged themselves politely on each side of the stage so as not to impede the view. The low clouds above the mountain rose, the last of the obstructing shutters slid out of the way, " and the King's Majesty and the rest of the masquers were discovered sitting in the throne of Honour, his Majesty highest in a seat of gold, and the rest of the Lords about him."

There they stood, in their bluebell doublets, like the King's, their white stockings, their silver hats and ostrich feathers: in the midst Charles himself, looking for once a great deal larger than life, for the sharply narrowing perspective of Inigo Jones's sets made no allowance for the actual size of the performers who were to appear backstage. Larger than life, therefore, and very regal, he sat, with his cousin Lennox on his right, and the Earl of Carlisle on the left, tall young men with fair, horsy, well-bred faces; six other lords were ranged at suitable distances round about. Instantly the Beloved People broke into laudatory song.

> *Since strength of virtues gained you Honour's throne*
> *Accept our wonder and enjoy our praise!*
> *He's fit to govern there, and rule alone,*
> *Whom inward helps, not outward force, doth raise.*

Certainly King Charles's throne rested on no effective outward force in spite of his present efforts to remedy the deficiency. But at the moment the spectators were not paying much attention to the words even if they could distinguish them. The King's throne, lords and all, had been slowly lowered to ground-level; he rose and at the same time there appeared, high up under the cornice, the largest and most solid of the many clouds which had yet descended from the pulleys in the heavens. " A huge cloud of various colours," Inigo Jones described it. It was indeed vast, since it concealed—or, to maintain the illusion, it carried— no less than eleven people. As it reached mid-air and mid-stage, it was seen slowly to open, revealing " a transparent brightness of thin exhalations." " Tinsel " is the word scribbled on Inigo Jones's sketch, but it is possible that the rays which broke from the cloud were not all tinsel. There may have been light effects managed by reflectors, for Inigo Jones fancied himself at tricks of the kind. Whatever the nature of the " transparent brightness," in the heart of it among her " martial ladies " sat the Queen herself.

When the ladies were rehearsing for the masque, the Earl of Northumberland wrote to his sister that they were the worst set of faces he had ever seen on such an occasion. But he was pre-judiced; neither of his own sisters—one the celebrated beauty Lady Carlisle—had been chosen. If their portraits are to be trusted against his word, they were a pretty enough collection. There was the sweet-faced Duchess of Lennox, exchanging eye-signals with her husband on the King's right: they were deeply in love. There was the lymphatic blonde, Lady Carnarvon, a convinced Puritan who had stipulated that she would only appear in the Queen's masque if it was not performed on a Sunday. There was the handsome, headstrong Lady Newport, carrying her sorrows with a high head; no eye-signals here although Lord Newport stood opposite her close by the King. He was the Puritan of this marriage and her adoption of the Roman Catholic religion a year or two back had done more than the bearing of three imbecile children to alienate him from her for ever. There was the glowing bride, Lady Kinalmeaky, whom the King himself had given away three weeks before.

But the Queen herself drew all eyes. In looks she hardly competed with the younger women who surrounded her. She was thirty years old and pregnant for the ninth time. She had lost her looks in her first childbed and was in the habit of saying —judging all other cases from her own—that no woman was beautiful after eighteen. She was a scrawny little woman with an ivory skin, a figure slightly twisted, features too large for the meagre face, and teeth which, as a niece once unkindly said, protruded from her mouth like guns from a fortress. But the King worshipped her and he was not the only one. Plain, old before her time, in wretched health, she dominated her younger and handsomer ladies by the electric animation of her personality. Her prominent eyes sparkled; when her thin, long mouth parted into a smile it was a chord of music. So she sat, mistress of stage and Court, from her throne in the multi-coloured cloud, a diminutive figure in carnation silk with plumed helmet and scarlet baldric and an antique sword at her side, the undoubted Queen of the Amazons.

As her cloudy car touched the ground the King advanced, took her by the hand and led her in procession from the stage to the place where her mother sat among the audience. The lords and ladies sought their wives or the partners allotted to them and followed in stately dance.

The King and Queen were now seated in the midst of the Court, but it remained for the Beloved People to sing a final salutation. For the last time all the handles were being turned off-stage; for the last time the clouds laboured up and down. For the last time the pictured cloths opened to reveal the last backdrop. It was the noblest and most elaborate of all Inigo Jones's effects and his sketch-books show that he had drawn it time and time again before he was satisfied. The scene was one of " magnificent buildings composed of several pieces of architecture. In the farthest part was a bridge over a river, where many people, coaches, horses and such like were seen to pass to and fro: beyond this, on the shore were buildings in perspective, which shooting far from the eye showed as suburbs of a great city." The whole represented, by implication, the King's extensive building programme in London to which Inigo Jones himself had so largely contributed. He did not, of course, go so far as to include actual drawings of the Piazza at Covent Garden or the new west front of St. Paul's Cathedral—the bridge was frankly modelled on a recent new bridge in Rome—but only the slowest courtier could fail to take his meaning. Here, almost as large as life, was the final representation of the blessings which King Philogenes had poured upon his Beloved, and strangely ungrateful, People.

For the moment the menacing discontent of England and Scotland, the cabals and intrigues of the King's enemies, the rude things that his people wrote on walls and sometimes even in pamphlets, were forgotten. On the final chords of Louis Richard's long-lost music three more cloudy chariots jerked across the sky above the city and opened to reveal all the musicians playing on their instruments to present the music of the spheres. Last of all, in the centre of the stage " the heavens opened full of deities which celestial prospect, with the Chorus below, filled the whole scene with apparitions and harmony." In the general exclamation of the audience, the merry accompaniment of the fiddlers, the creaking of the mechanism, Davenant's words may not have been altogether distinguishable. The Beloved People vociferously saluted the wisdom of their reigning King.

> *All that are harsh, all that are rude,*
> *Are by your harmony subdued,*
> *Yet so into obedience wrought*
> *As if not forced to it, but taught.*
> *Live still, the pleasure of our sight*
> *Both our example and delight . . .*

Inigo Jones was delighted with his effects. By his own account they were " generally approved of, especially by all strangers that were present, to be the noblest and the most ingenious that hath been done here in that kind." The one other opinion that has come down to us is markedly different. Young Robert Read, nephew of one of His Majesty's principal Secretaries of State, wrote some days later to his cousin Tom Windebanke in Ireland. " The mask was performed last Tuesday night, myself being so wise as not to see it. They say it was very good, but I believe the disorder was never so great at any."

There was room for disorder among all those pulleys and cog-wheels, those ascending and descending chariots and clouds, those quadruple scene changes. Which windlass jammed while the stage-hands strained at the handle, what backdrop stuck as it went up, leaving the scene half-cornfield and half-stormy sea? Did the Beloved People like sheep go astray all over the stage? For a moment the imagination pictures the frantic, furtive signals, the forgotten cue whispered in agitation, the audience sometimes restive, sometimes laughing, and the vacant eyes of Marie de Medici, vaguely aware of compliment, but blind to meaning.

The allegory of tempest giving place to joyous calm, of

Philogenes bestowing peace on his applauding people, was defiantly inept. Among the eight blue-and-silver lords about the King there were three at least who vehemently opposed his policy in public, and among the rest not one who did not conceal a dark anxiety under the radiant *mine de circonstance* demanded by the part. Young Lennox, who nine years later was to offer vainly to die in his master's place, knew well and feared the temper of his countrymen in the north. The bewildered Earl of Lanark, a lip-biting, over-burdened, conscientious young man, had in the last few days been presented with the impossible appointment of Secretary of State for rebellious Scotland. Among the English lords there were Russell and Fielding who were well aware from their Puritan kinsmen and friends that the King's reputation in England had never stood so low—an indignant city, a restive gentry, a depressed and uneasy people. The accidental disorders on the stage added their unintentional, tacit note of satire to the last masque ever to be danced by King Charles.

The last chorus ended, the clustered wax candles were lighted in all the sconces, the musicians from their cloudy gallery began to play again, the masquers mingled with the audience and the King and Queen danced among their courtiers. The rhythmic patter and swish of the dancing feet, the hum of voices, the susurration of silks, filled for the last time the Queen's great Dancing Barn.

Beyond the precincts of Whitehall, skewering rashers of bacon from the glowing coals of their winter fires, or warming knotted hands at the blaze of wood and the glow of turf, the people of England in town and country talked of their own affairs, made love or made baskets, darned the day's tears in worn clothes, smoked a pipe of tobacco or took a pot of ale after the day's work, before huddling by families on to their flock mattresses to sleep. A few were talking politics, more than a few were praying. The revolving world carried the island and all on it through the darkness to the late winter dawn and brought nearer by one day that January morning nine years in the future, when King Charles, haggard and dignified, would enact outside Whitehall the last scene in the story of Philogenes.

CLARENDON, in his *History of the Rebellion and Civil Wars in England*, states that the disturbances in Scotland which preceded the Bishops' Wars came as a shock to the English councillors of King Charles I. It seems probable that they came as a shock to King Charles himself. The unexampled authority that his father James VI had succeeded in establishing for the Crown in Scotland—an authority which he continued to exercise at long range when he became King of England—was something which Charles I had learnt to take for granted.

His father, addressing his English Parliament in 1607, had announced with pardonable satisfaction:

" Thus I must say for Scotland and may truly vaunt it: here I sit and govern it with my pen: I write and it is done: and by a Clerk of the Council I govern Scotland now, which others could not do by the sword."

There were signs of a weakening in this authority before King James died, if only in the steady increase of lawlessness on the Borders and in parts of the Highlands. But the dominion of the Crown over the major part of the kingdom still appeared intact.

It was therefore all the more startling to his son when the challenge to the royal authority first began to assume a violent form in Scotland, where he had least expected it to do so. Still less had he expected his English subjects to make common cause with his Scottish subjects against him. These two miscalculations first as to his power in Scotland and secondly as to the state of popular feeling between Scots and English, were fatal to him not only in Scotland but, as it turned out, in England as well.

The consideration of these errors and their possible causes was the starting-point of this enquiry into Anglo-Scottish relations between the union of the kingdoms and the breakdown of the personal rule of King Charles I.

Three phases may be distinguished in the span of thirty-five years which divides the Union of the Crowns from the signing of the National Covenant and the outbreak of revolt in Scotland. First there was the initial short phase during which the King and his two councils, Scottish and English, worked earnestly towards the closer union of the two countries. This phase came to an end when the projected scheme for the Union met with the vehement opposition of the English House of Commons. Since it had become apparent, during the negotiations, that the scheme was almost equally distasteful to both countries, King James abandoned the idea for the remainder of his reign, the only significant move during this second quiescent phase being the reorganization of the Scottish Privy Council, which began with the accession of King Charles I in 1625 and entered on the acute stage which led to the revolt with the King's visit to Scotland in 1633. During this period it was commonly believed that the reorganization of the Scottish Church was to be a step towards its amalgamation with the English Church and that this was in turn to lead on towards a closer union of the two nations. Whether this was true or not, the curious paradox remains that the King's policy, by bringing into being the same kind of opposition in both countries, did in fact bring his subjects of both nations much closer together than ever before, although not at all in the way he had intended.

To return to the first phase: the phase of open effort towards a closer Union of the Kingdoms. King James VI entered on his English inheritance with high and statesmanlike hopes, and also with that optimistic zeal which was one of his most endearing characteristics. He was aware of the technical and emotional problems which the new situation presented but was, it would appear, fully confident of his power to deal with them.

Speaking to the congregation assembled in St. Giles's on his last Sunday in Edinburgh before he left for England in April 1603, the King announced:

" My course must be . . . to establishe peace and religioun and wealth betwixt both the countries. And, as God has joynned the right of both the Kingdoms in my persoun, so yee may be joynned in wealth, in religioun, in hearts and effectiouns. And, as the one countrie has wealth, and the other has multitude of men, so we may part the gifts and everie one as they may doe to helpe other . . . And . . . as I have a bodie als able as anie King in Europ, whereby I am able to travell, so I sall vissie you everie three yeere at the least."

A year later, in July 1604, he set up a joint commission of both countries to draft a plan for the Union and in October he sent for the Scots Chancellor, the earl of Dunfermline, to London to assist in working it out. The King followed this by a pro-clamation ' dischairging and discontinewing the severall names of Scotland and England ' so that the ' hole island with the de-pendences and pertinentis of the same . . . sall keep in all ensewing ages the united denominatioun of the invincible monarchie of Greit Britane '. This alteration of two time-honoured names by no other authority than the royal prerogative was ill-received in both countries, where from that day to this the general term Great Britain and its colourless sub-division into North Britain and South Britain have never really penetrated into the vernacular. As for the Borders, they were, as the King had declared at Berwick on his journey to the south, ' borders ' no longer but ' the verie hart of the cuntrey ', and he was anxious to win a general acceptance for a term of his own invention, the ' Middle Shires ', as their new name. The inhabitants of the re-christened Middle Shires were requested in future to behave themselves " as becometh modest, quiet and peacable subjects, forbearing all violent, unlawful and extraordinar behaviour '. More than proclamations were, however, needed to control the borderers. Those on the Scottish side had celebrated the death of Queen Elizabeth and their King's accession to the English throne with a burst of renewed raiding over which Archbishop Spottiswoode in his *History* reproachfully shakes his head. ' The word no sooner come of the queen's death,' he states, ' than the loose and broken men in the borders assembling in companies made incursions upon England, doing what in them lay to divide the two Kingdoms.' The borders, placed under the control of the Scottish Privy Council, and provided with an efficient border police, did however now begin to make progress towards more peaceful conditions.

The joint flag which King James next designed to distinguish the ships of both nations at sea was badly received in Scotland because the cross of St. George was superimposed on the cross of St. Andrew, an arrangement which the King's Council ventured to suggest might ' breid some heat and miscontentment betwix your Majesteis subjects.'

It was found, when the proposed terms of a closer political and economic union were laid before the English Parliament in the winter of 1606-7, that there were more important things than flags to breed heat and miscontentment. The proposals for freedom of trade between the two countries and for the admission of Scots on equal terms into English trading companies struck against the vociferous and ill-mannered opposition of the English merchants.

The Scots, although more amenable, were on the whole relieved that the onus of opposing the King and preventing any closer union with the neighbour nation had been conveniently shouldered by the English. Although the Scottish Privy Council thought it necessary to object to the offensive tone of some of the speeches made in the House of Commons, there was a broad hint of relief in the letter which they sent to the King:

> " It is no littill greif to us to heir quhat just causes of discontentment are ministrat unto your Majestie at all these meetingis for enforceing that Union, *so greatlie hated by thame and so little affected by us,* except in that religious obedyence we aucht to your Majestie not to dislike onything that lykis you."

Their religious obedience, thanks to English opposition, was strained no further; the Scots Parliament passed the Union subject to its passage through the English Parliament as well, and in the English Parliament it suffered shipwreck.

A letter from the three Estates of the Scottish Parliament, when the danger was over in August 1607, has some significant phrases:

> " We nevir meant, to except aganis onie confounding as it

wer of these two before separated Kingdomes in one glorious monarchie and impyre of the whole Yle, bot onlie that this your Majesteis auncient and native Kingdome sould not be so disordourit and maid confusit by turneing of it, in place of a trew and friendlie Unioun, into a conquered and slavishe province to be governed by a Viceroy or Deputye, lyke suche of the King of Spaynes provinceis as your Majestie . . . made mentioun of."

The reference to Spain which James had made when expounding the Union to his English subjects had been singularly tactless to the Scots. The Spanish dependencies to which he had vaguely compared Scotland were Naples and Sicily; there was however a closer parallel in the situation which had arisen between Spain and the Netherlands, a parallel which would be rather too obvious to any reasonably well-informed Scottish statesman at the time. The Netherlands had first given a ruler to Spain, and in the early stages of this union of sovereignty the Spaniards had resented the influx of Netherlanders into their country and the overweight of Netherlandish councillors and favourites round their King, just as the English in the early years of James's reign were resenting Scottish influence at the court. In the following generation the tables were turned, and an entirely Spaniolated King had provoked the Netherlands to revolt by treating them as a province of Spain. This familiar sequence of events from comparatively recent history made Spain an unfortunate example for James to place before his subjects. There was therefore general relief when the Union was shelved and the technical readjustments between the two kingdoms with the one King were reduced to a minimum: namely, the repeal of all hostile laws, the mutual agreement not to harbour each other's criminals, and the ruling that the *post-nati* (those born *after* the King's accession) should be regarded as automatically naturalized citizens of both countries.

For the rest of his reign James left the Union question alone, and considerable care was exercised to prevent any infringement of the separate rights of either nation. The Scots Privy Council effectively silenced an English borderer who had tried to cite a Scot in the Star Chamber, and as late as 1632 we find a Scot referring a subpœna to appear before the English Exchequer to the Scots Privy Council lest by going to London in obedience to it he should create a precedent. The naturalization of Scots, born before the Union, who were elevated to English peerages was carried out by separate acts of Parliament for each case in the usual cumbrous way. In the opposite and rarer event of Englishmen being raised to Scottish peerages, it is not quite clear what, if anything, was regularly done. Viscount Falkland certainly became a naturalized Scot; but there seems to be no evidence either way as to whether Lord Fairfax of Cameron did so.

In so far as the King's policy of Union survived, it survived in his continued and drastic reorganization of the Scottish Church to bring it into line with the English one. But he handled the relationship between the two with considerable tact. There was, for instance, the important question of apostolic succession, which according to the Episcopalians had been broken in Scotland by the ascendancy of the non-episcopal Kirk. In England, apostolic succession, thanks to Cranmer, had been preserved intact. It was therefore evident that if the newly-appointed Scots bishops were to receive the laying on of hands in the correct manner, they must come to England for it. But the ceremony was not to be performed by the archbishops of Canterbury or York lest this should be held to imply that the Scottish Church was under the authority of either of these metropolitan sees. The bishops chosen to perform the ceremony were the bishops of Ely, Bath and London, whom one contemporary historian alleges to have been selected simply as 'the most ancient bishops' in England.

The precaution was essential, for even so obedient a servant of the King as John Spottiswoode, the archbishop of St. Andrews, felt very strongly on this point. A few years later he refused at the funeral of King James to take any other place in the procession except at the side of the archbishop of Canterbury. Having gained this point, he then found that he was expected to conform to English clerical customs and wear lawn sleeves. He refused and he was certainly within his rights, for the late King had regulated the apparel of Scottish bishops in considerable detail—coats of black damask, satin or velvet, and long gowns of velvet or other rich silk, and always 'their tippett of Spanishe taffetty about thair necks'. But when Spottiswoode failed to gain this second point, he refused to appear at the King's funeral, an act of a most unusual spirit from him which gained him the temporary favour of his compatriots, among whom he was not normally popular.

This second phase of King James's policy towards Scotland is marked by the slow decline of the power of his Council in that country. Before he died, his boast that he could govern Scotland with the pen was no longer absolutely true, and his son succeeded to a power, the foundations of which were already crumbling. The theoretical authority and the actual loyalty of the Scottish Privy Council were as strong as ever, but its prestige was dwindling.

The first signs of this diminished effectiveness are to be seen in the serious recrudescence of disorders in the Highlands and on the Borders, which marked the closing years of James's reign, and to which danger signals the King would undoubtedly have paid more heed had not the affairs of England come by this time to occupy the foreground of his attention.

The story of the Borders is particularly significant. The initial effort to turn the stormy debatable land into the peaceful Middle Shires had been extraordinarily successful. The iron gates of some of the border strongholds had been symbolically torn down and beaten into ploughshares and Sir William Cranstoun by a ruthless policy of hanging and deporting temporarily checked the activities of the reivers. One entire border clan, the Grahams, selected as an example no one quite knows why, was systematically exterminated by the destruction of their houses and the deportation of the men. In the year 1606 ' above a hundred and forty of the nimblest and most powerful thieves in all the border ' ended their lives on the gallows. Their names and nicknames in the reports of the Border Commissioners recall the days of heroic lawlessness commemorated in the ballads—Hob Armstrong of the Banks, Will Elliott called the Guide, Johnnie Noble called the Grip, Archie Milburne called Cold Archie, John Baty called Bide him Jock, and Andrew Armstrong, bastard son to Kinmont Willie, hero of the boldest rescue ever made from Carlisle castle, so much celebrated in local verse. Three years later the chancellor, Dunfermline, reported to the King with the utmost assurance that the Commissioners for the Borders had cleared them

" of all the chiefest malefactors, robbers and brigands as were wont to reign and triumph there, as clean . . . as Hercules sometime is written to have purged Augeas his ecuries . . . and has rendered all those ways and passages betwixt your Majesty's Kingdoms of Scotland and England as free and peacable as Phœbus in old times made free and open the ways to his own oracle at Delphos . . . These parts are now, I can assure your Majesty, as lawful, as peacable and as quiet as any part in any civil Kingdom in Christianity."

The peace of the Middle Shires lasted about ten years. In 1621 King James ill-advisedly dissolved the small armed guard which had been created to keep order in the district. The troops had not been gone a year before the reivers were as active as ever. 'Thift increases michtilie in Annanderdaile, Eskdaill, Ewisdaill, and in the nether pairtis of Nithisdaill', it was reported, 'the lymmaris ar so insolent and unreullie, because thair is not ane gaird . . . that thai cair not quhat thai do, and sa in this waise the cuntrie is wraikit in all pairtis.' A new joint Commission for the Borders was hastily set up, but it lacked the necessary backing of force and the country appears to have dropped steadily back into its endemic disorders. By 1635 an organized band of brigands was terrorizing almost the whole of the Borders. They are described as leading about

" as well by day as by night ane armed power to attempt and committ diverse wicked and lewde attempts . . . by ill using, assaulting, wounding, mayming and wickedlie killing diverse of our subjects and others, robbing and spoyling of their goods and some taking and imprissoning and in prison keeping in extreme hunger and cold even unto death, untill they sall make great and greevous fynes for the redemptioun of their persons, and also committing murthers, manslaughters, burglereis, ravishementis, robreis, felloneis, waists, besides burning of houses and barnes full of corne . . . and minassing and threatning with panes of life and death all such as sall in our courts of justice prosecute anie of the offenders for the offences foresaid."

Thus all that seemed to have happened on the Borders, until their local disturbances are submerged in the general agitation of the Civil Wars, was that the old border raiding with certain tacit rules and chivalries had given place to the ganging together of a ruthless dispossessed banditti.

The same disintegration of authority is visible in the Highlands and Islands. King James had initiated an extensive onslaught on Highland disorders and on the Highland way of life in general before he left Scotland. The famous outlawry of the entire MacGregor clan, who were thus handed over to the mercy of the Campbells and the Colquhouns, was dated the same week that he departed for England. The MacLeods of Lewis were coolly dispossessed to make way for a company of gentlemen adventurers from Fife who saw possibilities of developing the island. That extraordinary chieftain, Patrick, Earl of Orkney, himself an illegitimate kinsman of the royal family, who with a brood of illegitimate brothers and sons had established virtually a separate power in Orkney, deriving its revenues from piracy, was executed, with one of his sons, in Edinburgh. Meanwhile, a small naval expedition had been sent against the Western Isles and the major chiefs, having been kidnapped during a dinner-party on board one of the King's ships, the able and wily bishop of the Isles, Andrew Knox, persuaded those that were left to subscribe the Statutes of Icolmkill, a programme for the pacification of the Isles in which the chiefs agreed, among other things, to send their eldest sons to be educated in the Lowlands. The King had, at the same time, continued his policy of settling the blood feuds of the northern nobility by a system of compulsory marriages between the leading families.

But in the second and third decades of the century the disorders began to multiply again. The MacLeods proved altogether too much for the gentlemen adventurers from Fife, whose survivors twice beat a retreat before what the contemporary poet Lithgow has called, 'the desperate courage of these awful Hebrideans,' twice came back, and finally sold their rights to the Mackenzies, thus leaving the 'awful Hebrideans' to fight it out between themselves. Beyond the immediate sphere of Campbell control, in the Western Highlands, the Camerons and the Mackintoshes were again carrying on furious warfare. In 1624 the murder of two of the Gordons by the Crichtons of Frendraught undid years of pacifying work in the Eastern Highlands. When King Charles visited Scotland in 1633, the Privy Council commanded the 'principalls and chiftans of the clans in the Yles' to repair to Edinburgh to greet the King and to prove to the English visitors 'that the most remote part of this Kingdome and Yles thairof ar settled under ane perfyte obedience and peace.' The demonstration was a necessary piece of window dressing, for the power of the Privy Council to establish even the most imperfect obedience and peace was by this time more than doubtful. An outrageous case of wrecking on the coast of Lewis in the ensuing year seems to have gone quite unpunished.

The decline in the prestige and therefore in the power of the Scots Privy Council which had begun under James VI was unintentionally accelerated by Charles I. It was not the least of this King's misfortunes that he was always too much of a Scotsman for England and too much of an Englishman for Scotland. In many ways he was the type of the absentee Scot, rootless in England and uprooted from Scotland, a type which the circumstances of the Union of the Crowns had made very frequent about the English Court. He surrounded himself from choice with men of the same kind: the Duke of Lennox, the Marquis of Hamilton, Will Murray. In this way he created for himself the illusion of being in touch with Scottish feeling when in fact he had lost contact with it.

The Council which James VI had left to carry out his will in Scotland had been well chosen, in the King's own eloquent phrase, of such men as he could correct or were hangable. But they did also sufficiently represent the prestige and power of the Scots lords. Having created such a Council, he let it alone, merely filling the vacancies as they occurred. Charles I, a young man with ideas but no experience and very little acquired knowledge of Scottish politics, tampered incessantly both with the organization and the composition of the Council. He reconstituted it shortly after his accession, insisting on the exclusion of any members who were also Lords of Session. This not only removed men with the kind of legal experience and standing necessary on the Council, but also incapacitated its most assiduous attenders, because the judges only had to cross the road to reach the Council Chamber. Charles then, contrary to all advice, fixed too large a quorum. No king with an elementary knowledge of the transport problems of Scotland could have made so simple a mistake, particularly after excluding all those who found attendance easy. His subsequent steady appointment of the bishops to seats on the Council was chiefly intended to forward his Church policy, against which, especially the revocation of all grants of church land to laymen since the Reformation, the Council had at first warmly protested. He may also have believed that clerics, with no family lands demanding their attention, could be relied on to devote themselves more exclusively to the work of the Council. But the very frequent changes that he made in its personnel produced an atmosphere of fidgets and intrigue very unsuitable to the conduct of affairs.

Thus, in creating what he thought would be a wholly obedient

Council, Charles lost sight of the one essential, that it should also be an efficient Council, a united, respected and powerful body. He was to find when he came to impose his Church policy, that the Council was willing but was impotent. He had fatally lessened its prestige and its effectiveness by omitting too many of the Scots lords who felt they had a right to sit on it. The most extraordinary omission was probably that of the young Earl of Montrose whose father had been on the Council for over twenty years, whose grandfather had been chancellor and whose family tradition had been one of service to the Crown for the past century. The appointment of a coming young man of this background ought to have been automatic. There were other less startling instances of the same kind. The effect of such omissions was to create exactly what James VI had been most careful to avoid, namely a focus of discontent, combined with power and prestige, *outside* the Council. Thus at the same time Charles weakened his own Council and set up rival factions. In the course of his royal visit in 1633 Charles moreover added nine Englishmen to the Council in Scotland. These appointments were scarcely more than nominal, as the English were unlikely to be present again in Scotland after the royal visit, and moreover Charles might fairly have argued that the number of Scots with official appointments in England far outweighed the number of Englishmen with appointments in Scotland. Nevertheless this dilution of the Council by nominal members who were ignorant of Scots affairs was not calculated to strengthen its prestige.

This treatment of the Council is worth emphasizing, for nationalist resentment in Scotland—not so much against the English partner-nation, as against an absentee monarch—was steadily growing. The promise made by King James of revisiting his native land every three years had not been kept. He came back only once, in 1617; King Charles postponed his first visit until 1633—eight years after his accession. The loss to the smaller towns which had counted on the almost annual visits of their King to bring a bustle of visitors and trade was considerable. Perth was described by John Taylor the Water-poet as early as 1618 as being 'much decayed, by reason of the want of his Majesty's yeerely comming to lodge there'. William Lithgow in his flowery welcome to King Charles in 1633 puts into the mouth of Scotland lines suitable to a deserted wife:

> *True, and most true it is, the Proverbe proves,*
> *That age is still injur'd, by younger loves:*
> *And so am I, thine eldest Region made,*
> *A prey to dark oblivion's winter shade.*

It was thus with a weakened Council and with a nation acutely sensitive to the fact that their King preferred his other kingdom that Charles set out to complete his father's work and bring Scotland into religious conformity with England. Strong as was the purely religious element in the opposition which gathered against him, the nationalist element must not be underestimated.

Charles made a certain allowance for national feeling; but as it turned out, not nearly enough. The popularly miscalled Laudian liturgy, the new Service Book which he attempted to introduce in 1637, was in fact largely a Scottish compilation, and the bishops on whom Charles relied to introduce it in Scotland—Spottiswoode, Sydserf and the spirited Whitford, who read it with a pair of pistols on the pulpit in front of him—were pure Scots by birth, breeding and education. A certain amount of care had thus been taken by the King not to offend Scottish susceptibilities; but he lacked the imagination to see that his precautions needed to go far deeper. He could not wipe out the cumulative effect of his own and his father's absences, of the English appointments to the Privy Council, of the bustling up and down to London of the Scots bishops charged with the preparation of the Prayer Book. A sense of neglect and long-pent-up national resentment were strongly mingled with the religious feeling which caused the riots in Edinburgh at the introduction of this ' Popish-English-Scottish-Mass-Service-Book '. The document of protest drawn up by the opposition and largely managed by the noblemen whom Charles had deliberately and mistakenly kept off the Council, was significantly named the *National* Covenant.

This was, however, nationalism with a difference. The Scots were perfectly well aware that there was considerable opposition to the King's religious policy in England. They were careful to prepare an *Information for all Good Christians within the Kingdom of England* setting forth their case to possible sympathizers south of the border. King Charles for his part found when it came to a war with the Scots that, for perhaps the first time in history, the English were not prepared to fight even to prevent an invasion, so deeply were they infected with sympathy for the Scots revolt.

The royal miscalculation was not wholly inexplicable. King Charles seems to have made the mistake of judging the relations between the two peoples exclusively from the official knowledge he had of them, a knowledge based on the narrow limits of his own court and the various official disputes which came to his notice. Officially Anglo-Scottish relations had often been strained, and had never been really cordial since the Union of the Crowns.

The joining together of two nations of which one was incomparably the wealthier had been bound to produce some unhappy consequences. The English resented the influx of Scottish adventurers of all classes, and the Scots resented the English assumption that their commercial interests should always have the first consideration. The Union plan had broken down because English merchants would not admit Scots merchants to equal privileges with themselves, and although the Scots were glad enough that the plan had broken down, they resented the reason. Later there had been ugly disputes about the allotment of land in Nova Scotia, incontrovertibly started as a Scottish colony; English adventurers had quite shamelessly attempted to get the charter to the Scots cancelled in their favour. Again the Greenland Company of London not only trespassed in waters to which the Scots had been granted a prior right, but, in 1629, the Scots complained, ' seazed upon thair chellps, medled with all the provisioun being thairin, and have takin thair men prisonners and used thame with all rigour, sua that the shippes quhilks wer reiked furth for that voyage at ane verie great charge ar now returned emptie, to the heavie loss and discouragement of the undertakers.'

In commerce the English undoubtedly had the whip hand and used it. Thus when the Scots, perturbed at the alarming increase in the consumption of English beer—a brew which had become astonishingly more fashionable than any native one —tried to keep it out by putting up the duty against it, the English instantly retaliated with a threat to raise the duty on wool and coal, the two chief Scottish exports, a counterblow which, if it had been put into effect, would have been disastrous to Scottish trade. However, an attempt by the English some years later, in 1623, to compel the Scots to sell all their raw wool exclusively to England was successfully resisted on the ground that a monopoly of this kind would enable the English to fix the price as they liked. Rumours and echoes of this foiled plan, so advantageous to the English, rumble on for some years; the Commission appointed to enquire into the depression in the English cloth trade in the early years of Charles I, for instance, reproachfully cites the sale of Scots wool to foreign manufacturers as one contributory cause of the English depression.

The English, for their part, saw very much the worst of the Scots during the early years of the century. It was evident that the more populous and more prosperous southern country offered better opportunities for the work-shy to pick up a livelihood. Gangs of sturdy beggars from Scotland soon found it worth their while to save enough to persuade friendly sea captains to set them down at convenient places on the English coast, whence they swarmed over the country in such quantities that it was necessary to issue five—evidently inadequate—prohibitions between 1606 and 1620 against the unlicensed carrying of ' beggarlie passengeris ' to England. The prohibitions were felt to be essential for the preservation of good social relations between the countries, lest, as one order of the Privy Council phrased it, the crowding of ' idill suitaris and uncomelie people ' into England should give an impression that there were ' no persones of good rank, comlynes nor credite ' in Scotland. Certainly the tone of some English lampoons on the Scots at this date do suggest that this was the impression made. A further order commanded all recruited soldiers going from Scotland to Europe to go direct by sea and not to cross over England, where the unruly behaviour of groups of Scots asserting themselves to be soldiers travelling to foreign wars ' procures the privat grudge and miscontentment of the people of that land against his Majesteis subjectis of this kingdome '.

King James himself was aware of the psychological difficulties presented by the arrival of a Scottish king with Scots courtiers in England. To do him justice—and he is a king to whom less

than justice is persistently done—he sent back the greater part
of his Scottish household servants as soon as he arrived in London
and found Queen Elizabeth's palaces already fully staffed with
Englishmen and women. His extreme liberality to his Scots
favourites he excused to the Parliament in 1607 with the endear-
ring phrase that both he and they had regarded the first three
years of his reign as a sort of Christmas. On the whole he made
a consistent effort to avoid or soften the jealousies which might
arise between the two nations at and around the court. Thus
when his eldest son was installed as Prince of Wales he created
only five Scottish Knights of the Bath to twenty Englishmen,
a very reasonable proportion.

The insults that the members of either nation lightly hurled at
the other were punished with considerable severity from time
to time. Balfour records with evident pleasure the execution
in Edinburgh of Thomas Ross, who had nailed up a number of
anti-Scottish theses on the door of the University Church in
Oxford and offered to defend them in disputation. An English
traveller who, in course of a heated dispute with a Scot in a ship,
lying off Civita Vecchia, was reported to have said that 'any
merchant in London was able to buy all Edinburgh' was called
up in front of the Council in London, where he protested that
he had only said 'some four merchants of London dealt for as
much merchandise as all Edinburgh did'.

King James would have liked men to believe that the English
had the monopoly of bad manners, and went so far as to assert
in an address to his English Parliament that no Scot had used
opprobrious terms of the English. The contrary seems, however,
to be proved by the existence of a Scottish act of Parliament of
1609 prohibiting the publication or uttering of 'pasquillis,
libellis, rymis, cokalanis, comedies and siclyk' against the
English.

It was in England, however, that the ill-feeling between the two peoples most often came to a violent expression, for the fairly obvious reason that while there was a nucleus of Scots to provoke national resentments in England and chiefly round London, there was no equivalent group of English in Scotland, where the visitors were few, were on the whole well-behaved, and were usually made very welcome.

The King was on the whole fairly faithfully supported by his courtiers and by his Scots and English Councils in preventing unnecessary trouble. There was the notorious incident in 1612 at Croydon races when a Scot named Ramsay hit the Earl of Montgomery in the face and the Earl of Montgomery failed to respond in kind, so that, as a contemporary sourly observed, there was ' nothing lost but the reputation of a gentleman '. Montgomery's friends asserted that he stomached the insult in order to prevent a free fight between Scots and English, and to be fair, it seems very probable that this was indeed his reason, though he never quite lived down having lost his reputation. Altogether the year 1612 was an uneasy time for Anglo-Scottish relations in London, and things very nearly came to an outburst again over the case of Lord Sanquhar who had hired a couple of assassins to murder an English fencing master who had accidentally put out his eye. None of his compatriots in high place, however, took Lord Sanquhar's part in the matter, and he was hanged, to the gratification of the English and to no regret of the Scots.

There is, however, one other aspect of the situation in and round the court which it is not out of place to consider here, because it has not been much noticed and it undoubtedly had a considerable effect on the position of the Crown in Scotland. The departure of the King had broken up the cadre of the Scottish court. What was created in England was essentially an

English court with a Scottish, or as time went on, an Anglo-Scottish enclave within it. Although such men as Hamilton and Lennox, the most outstanding examples of the anglicized Scots nobleman, were evidently men of high authority, the reputation in general of the anglicized Scots did not stand very high north of the Border. There certainly seems to have grown up a substantial group of Scots lords who preferred to disassociate themselves from their compatriots at the English court, which meant of course to disassociate themselves from the court altogether. Lord Gordon, for instance, who became Huntly in 1636, we find making long visits to the French court and comparatively short ones to the English, to which he almost deliberately did not belong. The same thing was significantly true of the young Montrose. This was a dangerous situation for the King to allow to grow up, because it was a bare generation since the Scots nobility had at last been gathered into some kind of order and allegiance under the Crown. To allow distinguished Scots peers to revert to an uninterrupted independence, and to feel not even the social magnetism of the court—let alone any other—was to increase the risk of ultimate rebellion.

Meanwhile more than thirty years of a common sovereignty had insensibly strengthened links between the Scottish and the English peoples of which the King, dealing only with the political surface, remained unaware. English travellers, with few exceptions messengers of goodwill, had been well received in Scotland and had acquired a respect for some at least of what they saw there. Both the prolific poet and journalist John Taylor in 1618 and Sir William Brereton in 1636 were awed by the physique of the Highlanders. Taylor, an irrepressible tourist, boldly penetrated as far as Braemar to join in the hunting, borrowed a kilt for the occasion from the kindly earl of Mar and can thus probably claim to have been the first but emphatically not the last Englishman to masquerade unconvincingly in borrowed romance. He was impressed too by the bounty of Scottish hospitality and the patriarchal households of the lairds who generously gave him lodging in the course of his tour.

Sir William Brereton's record of 1636, on the eve of the outbreak of the religious troubles, is more significant. Like Taylor, he was impressed by the patriarchal manners of the Scottish gentry to their families and servants. He also writes approvingly of the demonstrations which some congregations in Scotland had made against ministers who in accordance with the royal instructions had tried to introduce kneeling and other Popish ceremonies. It is evident, from the way in which he writes of these things and the introductions which he had, that the close connections which had once existed between the Reformed kirk in Scotland and the Elizabethan Puritans—Cartwright, it will be remembered, had been offered a chair at St. Andrews—had outlasted the Union of the Crowns and been strengthened by the fact that both were now equally exposed to attack from above.

But the forcing house of understanding between the two nations was neither in England nor in Scotland, but on the mainland of Europe. There had been very extensive recruiting in Scotland for the Protestant powers involved in the Thirty Years War. There was much volunteering from England. The muster rolls of Swedish, Dutch and Danish armies show interesting mixtures of names from both countries. In parenthesis, on the Catholic side, the murder of Wallenstein in 1634 must have been planned and carried out entirely in the English language between an Irish colonel, a Scottish colonel and an English major. But it was in the Protestant armies, especially the Dutch and Swedish, that bonds of personal friendship and above all of common religious convictions were being increasingly formed between the representatives of the two nations.

An influence of equal importance came from the English-speaking churches in the Netherlands. These seem to have been truly Anglo-Scottish, and were all of them closer to the Dutch Calvinist model than to the Anglican establishment to which they were only very vaguely attached. Their powers of ordination had long caused anxiety to the Anglican Church at home and they were the source of a steady trickle of ministers to both England and Scotland whose doctrines and practice were wholly at variance with the forms that Archbishop Laud was trying to impose. The dictates of the English Privy Council commanding them to conform to Anglican measures, were disregarded by them and were politely deprecated by the Dutch government under whose protection they existed. The Low Countries thus became the convenient resort of those who opposed the government on religious grounds, and it was here that the dissident godly of both nations made significant friendships.

To all of this King Charles was insufficiently alive, although his opponents seem to have been perfectly aware of it. The English sympathy for the Scots revolt early caused the moving spirit of the National Covenant, Lord Rothes, to note piously that ' some growth of Christian affection amongst neighbours may prove this cord to be twisted by a hand from above', meaning presumably that God had taken a hand in bringing English and Scots together against the church policy of their common King.

Thus in the first thirty-five years of the Union of the two countries under one sovereign, the King's attempts to achieve either an economic or a religious union, by policy directed from the centre, had both broken down: the first on English resentment, the second on Scottish intransigence. The first real movement of mutual help and affection between the two peoples was created not by the policy of the Crown but by resistance to it. It is an interesting and possibly an instructive paradox.

# THE CAUSES OF THE CIVIL WAR

TWO SEPARATE but related questions have to be answered about the conflict that divided England in the middle years of the seventeenth century. What was the nature of the crisis in English government at this time? Could that crisis have been resolved without war, and if not why not?

The conflict had two aspects—it was concerned with problems of government peculiar to England, but it was also a part of the religious wars that affected the whole of Western Europe for a century after the Reformation. In so far as the crisis concerned the internal affairs of England, it might have been resolved peacefully. But the dynastic and religious conflict, at that time dividing Europe, introduced elements into the English situation that transformed a political and administrative struggle into a military one.

The political and religious causes of the war are those that have been traditionally emphasized. The King, in common with most European sovereigns of the time, wished to strengthen the central government and was impatient of the hindrances put in his way by Parliament and by the gentry who exercised local power. The gentry, in and out of Parliament, resented interference with what they believed to be their liberties and privileges. This constitutional struggle was intensified by religious feeling. It was a logical part of the King's centralizing policy to insist on uniform religious practices and submission to the state Church.

But many of his subjects inclined, with varying degrees of fervour, towards forms of Protestantism which could not, or would not, be included within the Anglican Church. The religious and political opposition to the Crown thus came into very close association.

This is the broad outline of the political picture presented by England in the first half of the seventeenth century. Many details can be added to it, to strengthen and modify the general impression, but it is important to remember that such details are *additions*: they do not basically alter the general situation.

It is usual to emphasize the poverty of the Crown and Parliament's control of subsidies as a cause of tension between King and Commons in this epoch, and as a principal reason for the failure of King Charles's experiment in non-Parliamentary government. Certainly the King lacked funds for the effective exercise of power; but it was the lack of government officials, quite as much as the lack of funds, that wrecked the monarchy. King Charles during his personal rule found numerous subterfuges for raising money. Had he developed his industrial and monopoly programme more consistently and more thriftily, had he allowed his courtiers less latitude and his financial advisers more, it is conceivable that he might have solved the money problem at least as effectively as any of his contemporaries abroad.

It was not lack of money that prevented him from quelling the revolt of the Scots in 1639 and 1640. Twice over, with or without money, he got an army together and marched it to the North. But the spirit was lacking. The men were deplorably bad material: " all the rogues in the kingdom," said Sir Jacob Astley; and they were very unwilling to fight. What undermined the King's policy much more than lack of funds was lack of co-operation. Strafford, the King's chief minister, spoke of " a general disaffection to the King's service." Among those responsible for recruiting, equipping and sending the troops, from Lords Lieutenants to Justices of the Peace, the majority shared in this " general disaffection." They were at worst hostile to the King's policy, at best bored with it, and their behaviour varied from the indifferent to the actively obstructive. They had neither faith in nor respect for the King's government. The King's government, for its part, had very limited powers of coercion against them, for the simple reason that no other body of men existed to replace them. The King could not get rid of obstructive Justices of the Peace and put in loyal ones, because there were at that time simply not enough loyal gentlemen to be found. When the Short Parliament met, in April 1640, great efforts were made in Yorkshire, under the influence of Strafford, to send devoted King's men as M.P.s to Westminster. As a result the county was for over a month almost entirely denuded of loyal King's men, the obstructionists had it all their own way at home, while the loyalists, who could not be in two places at once, were serving the King at Westminster. This desperate shortage of support was fatal to the royal administration.

That was the cardinal weakness of King Charles's government. He had no civil service, no country-wide bureaucratic class dependent on him. The royal policy, divulged by proclamation, depended for its implementation on local men, principally on the Justices. These were not officials exclusively dependent on the Crown but gentlemen of standing in their own right who had, over the years, developed their own traditions of behaviour and their own views on what was good for the country—and for themselves. If a majority of them felt no enthusiasm for the policies of the Crown, as far as these affected the internal life of the country, then the policies of the Crown would not be carried out.

In theory, King Charles understood the necessity of controlling

183

the Justices, who were required to report regularly to the central government. But he failed to realize what Queen Elizabeth had always known, that in practice his powers depended on making his policies acceptable to those who were to enforce them. Thus, when it came to the Scots war, the troops were well aware that the gentry, who had unwillingly scraped them together, were no more interested in the war than they were themselves. Desertion, indiscipline and mutiny followed naturally from this knowledge.

A situation had arisen in which government became impossible as soon as the King found himself at loggerheads with the gentry. He had the authority to initiate and plan a policy, but he had not the power to enforce it. The gentry had the power to enforce (or not to enforce) a policy, but had not the power to initiate it. Such a situation could not last. One of two things was bound to happen: either the King had to find means to enlarge an official class dependent on himself—the solution found by Richelieu and most of the European absolutists: or the gentry had to find means of controlling the initiation of policy, so that they would only be required to do what they were willing to do.

A centralizing government policy, whether in Church or State, is quite naturally and inevitably unpopular with those who are accustomed to exercising local power and local discretion, and who do not wish to see their power (or their rights, as they would say) invaded. But this explanation for the opposition to King Charles I has of recent years been felt to be inadequate. It has been suggested that the real cause for the opposition was economic—that the dominant gentry were rich and growing richer, and were consequently irritated at the Crown's medieval interventions in favour of common good and the common people against private profiteering and the unrestricted operation of the capitalist system. Conversely, it is argued that the trouble was caused not by the rich gentry at all, but by the poor gentry: that the epoch was one of economic recession, and that the instability of the gentry's position, and that of landed society in general, caused the unrest that led to war.

Evidence can be found for both these arguments, and this is not in the least surprising since many different reasons for economic unrest did undoubtedly exist in the England of King Charles. The very plentiful surviving evidence by no means lends itself to straightforward interpretation and has hardly yet been fully assembled from all possible sources. The economic policy of King Charles was, in any case, so inconsistent that it was likely to arouse protest—as it did—from almost all types of men. At one moment, he was fining depopulators and profiteers in the interests of the poor; at another, he was encouraging them. At one moment, he was protecting the interests of the cottager against the engrossing landowner, at another, shovelling cottagers and squatters out of the way for the benefit of shareholders in agricultural or industrial schemes, or to improve his deer parks, or simply to raise money by fines. He did whatever suited him at the moment. Thus economic motives for opposition to his policies are all-pervasive, but they are—like the policies themselves—of many different kinds.

The crisis, however, was not in essence an economic crisis. It was a political and administrative crisis. The critical position of the gentry did not arise from their economic power—or lack of it—but from their administrative power. That, and that above all, made a constitutional upheaval of some kind inevitable. The Long Parliament, which met in November 1640, solved the problem by putting through legislation against the prerogative Courts, thus curtailing the coercive powers of the Crown, and arrogated to themselves the right to coerce opponents, and to discuss and, by implication, to initiate policy. At this point, the constitutional revolution was complete *without a war*. What turned a peaceful revolution into a shooting war was the European situation, the strategic position of the British Isles and the King's foreign policy.

In Europe, wars of religion had been almost continuous since the Reformation. Under Queen Elizabeth I, England had come to play the part that the majority of her educated people thought the right one—against Roman Catholic Spain, in favour of the Protestant powers and their allies. This policy was natural to a people who were predominantly Protestant, and whose overseas expansion had already brought them into collision with Spain. The fact that John Pym, leader of the Commons in 1640, a strong Puritan, was also secretary of the Providence Company, with its trading interests in the Caribbean, has been often and rightly emphasized. On the European mainland the Habsburg dynasty (Spain-Austria) had made themselves the defenders of the Roman Catholic Church and had, by force of arms, undone the work of the Reformation in Bohemia and much of South Germany. By 1629, when King Charles was on the eve of his experiment in non-Parliamentary government, the imperial Roman Catholic armies reached the Baltic. This menacing background to the English situation is too often overlooked. The Protestant Cause—which, in a vague way, meant a great deal to many Englishmen—was in a very depressed state when King Charles's personal rule began.

In the triumphant advance of the imperial Catholic forces, King Charles's brother-in-law, the Protestant Elector Palatine who had rashly accepted the Crown of Bohemia from Protestant rebels of that country, had become a landless and homeless exile. It was a source of frequent, if often uninformed and unreasonable, criticism of King Charles, that he had done far too little for his brother-in-law, and after his death, for his widow and children. But the King's sins of omission were less glaring than his sins of commission. Spain was the other half of the Spanish-Austrian Habsburg combine; and Spain was the traditional enemy and rival of England. It is true that, by the sixteen-thirties, Spain was a much weakened power and, in some sort, rather the traditional than the actual villain of the piece.

English merchants were beginning to look with equal resentment on the rising power of the Dutch. But the re-orientation of opinion was far from complete. The Spaniards still barred English expansion in the new world, especially in the Caribbean, while Dunkirk, in Spanish control, was a constant menace to English shipping. The Spaniards, for their part, needed the friendship of the English government, if they were to pursue their eighty years war with the Dutch. A hostile England would threaten the sea route of their money and troops for the Netherlands; a friendly England could give them help and protection against the growing menace of Dutch sea power in the Channel and the Narrow Seas.

In return, therefore, for considerable financial benefits King Charles had given help and protection to the Spaniards. All through the 'thirties Spanish bullion, for the payment of their troops in the Netherlands, was shipped in English ships by way of London to Antwerp. English ships, being technically neutral, were immune from attacks by the Dutch. In this way, King Charles's government gave valuable aid to Spanish arms against the Protestant Cause. In 1639, when with the loss of Breisach the Spaniards became unable to send their troops overland by the Rhine route into Flanders, King Charles allowed them to send them by sea in English ships. The Dutch, at last exasperated too far, stopped some of these ships; whereupon, to make it easier for the Spaniards, the King allowed them to land their men at Plymouth, march them overland and ship them again from Dover. Not more than a few thousand Spanish troops came in this way, but the operation was sufficiently noticeable to provoke rumours that the King—then at the height of his effort to force Anglican ritual upon the Calvinist Scots—was in league with Catholic Spain, and intended to subdue his Protestant subjects with the help of Spanish troops. Indeed, the whole Scots war was seen by many, in the British Isles and abroad, as the signal for Great Britain to become involved in the European conflict. The Scots would be supported by the Dutch and French, the King by the Spaniards; thus the dynastic-religious wars of Europe would be extended to our shores.

In the autumn of the same year, 1639, after the armistice with the Scots at Berwick, a Spanish Armada was chased into English territorial waters, where it was effectively destroyed by the Dutch Admiral, Marten Tromp. In this conflict, the English fleet did nothing; but the King, before the battle, had allowed the Spaniards to replenish their stores of gunpowder at a price, and he had given orders for the billeting of their troops on the ships in English coast towns, if they should be forced to land. All this looked very bad to his anti-Spanish Protestant subjects. A rumour that he was about to lease the southern Irish ports to the Spaniards as naval bases was, in the circumstances, very widely believed. It was only forty years since the Spaniards had actually occupied Kinsale; and, as events were soon to show, they had still considerable interest in gaining a foothold in southern Ireland for the defence of their sea routes. Whatever the King intended about the southern Irish ports, it is beyond question that, in the summer of 1640, Strafford tried, in his master's name, to arrange a loan of four million ducats from

Spain, in return for a regular guard of thirty-five ships of the English navy to convoy Spanish transports through the Channel. Nothing came of this, because the Dutch made it clear that they would consider the arrangement a breach of neutrality; and, much as Charles needed Spanish gold, he could not at that moment risk a Dutch war.

This was the background of recent foreign policy against which the English constitutional revolution took place. Charles had time and again shown himself to be not merely pro-Spanish but willing to accept Spanish subsidies and to give indirect help to Spanish arms in the European war, in defiance of the economic interests and the religious principles of a large majority of his subjects. In the autumn of 1641, revolt broke out in Ireland— a revolt of the Roman Catholic native population against Protestant Scottish and English settlers. This revolt was greatly stimulated by fear of what the powerful English Parliament, Protestant and anti-Spanish, might perpetrate in Ireland.

Irish exiles, both soldiers and priests, from the Spanish Nether- lands and Spain played a considerable part in the rising, so that the Irish rebellion was from the start associated with the European religious wars. Where did King Charles stand in this revolt? As King of England, he should have given the utmost of his protection to the Protestant settlers in Ireland. But the insurgents claimed that he had authorized them to act. He denied it, probably with a fair measure of truth; but his previous conduct gave strong colour to the insurgents' claim, and re-doubled the suspicions of Parliament. In the circumstances, Parliament insisted that the ultimate control of the forces to be raised for the suppression of the Irish revolt must lie with them. Suddenly, a dangerous constitutional question, which might otherwise have lain dormant, came into the forefront of debate: the question of the control of the armed forces. Since neither King nor Parliament would give way on this, civil war was the logical outcome.

Thus the immediate cause of the civil war was a clash over the control of the armed forces. This clash was the logical outcome of the suspicion engendered by the King's foreign policy. Without that suspicion there would have been nothing to make war inevitable or even likely. A constitutional struggle with legal weapons—that there must have been. But what converted a tussle in the law courts and Parliament to a violent clash of fighting men in the field was the state of religious and dynastic war on the continent, and the King's fatal espousal of what seemed to the majority of his subjects the wrong side. Without that, Parliament would hardly have dared to arrogate to itself the sovereign's right to defend his people. But Charles had shown that he was more interested in Spanish gold than in the immunity of British shores. This caused the Civil War.

# SOCIAL COMEDY IN THE REIGN OF
## CHARLES I

ON 2 September 1642 the London theatres were closed by an ordinance of the Lords and Commons, phrased in terms which would not have disgraced a tragedy:

"Whereas the distressed Estate of Ireland steeped in her own Blood and the distressed Estate of England threatened with a Cloud of Blood by a Civil Warre, call for all possible meanes to appease and avert the wrath of God appearing in these Judgments . . . and whereas publike Sports doe not well agree with publike Calamities, nor publike Stage playes with the Seasons of Humiliation, this being an Exercise of sad and pious solemnity, and the other being Spectacles of pleasure, too commonly expressing lascivious Mirth and Levitie: it is therefore thought fit and ordeined by the Lords and Commons in this Parliament Assembled, that while these sad Causes and set times of Humiliation doe continue publike Stage playes shall cease and bee forborne."

There was as much policy as moral reprobation in the decision of Parliament to close the theatres. Political and social comment, by no means always favourable to the government, had become increasingly common on the stage during the first half of the seventeenth century. During the Ship Money disputes Massinger had put these words into the mouth of a tyrannous King:

*Moneys? We'll raise supplies what ways we please,*
*And force you to subscribe to blanks in which*
*We'll mulct you as we shall think fit.*

Before the play was licensed the King marked this in the margin: 'This is too insolent and to be changed' so that the offending words never reached the public, but it is an interesting comment on the amount of liberty allowed to dramatists that Massinger introduced them at all. On other occasions the King's policy had come under open criticism from the theatre. During the religious troubles with Scotland the players at the Fortune Theatre introduced into one of their plays a mockery of the Laudian ritual which was received with great enthusiasm by the audience until the government prohibited the performance and confiscated the properties. Undeterred, the company retaliated by putting on a play called *The Valiant Scot* which dealt with the heroic resistance of Sir William Wallace to Edward I. The modern analogy was perfectly understood by the Londoners who sympathized with the Scots in their current rebellion against King Charles and the Laudian liturgy.

Since the accession of King Charles I the taste for topical comedy, immensely stimulated by Ben Jonson earlier in the century, had become fully established. Dramatists like the veteran Philip Massinger and Richard Brome, the one-time servant and assiduous imitator of Ben Jonson, as well as the fashionable James Shirley and a number of lesser men, both amateurs and professionals, made use of contemporary incidents and contemporary controversies in their comedies. Davenant, in his *Platonic Lovers* (1636), Brome in his *Court Beggar* (1632), Chapman and Shirley in *The Ball* (1632) exploited subjects of current interest and Thomas Heywood in *The Late Lancashire Witches* (1634) took his material almost unaltered from the

accounts of the famous witch trial in Lancashire in the previous
year. The realistic representation on the stage of familiar places
of public resort—as in Brome's *Covent Garden Weeded* and
Shirley's *Hyde Park* (1632)—underlined the contemporary character of stage comment on manners, morals and even politics.
The closing of the theatres was thus an obvious counsel of
prudence on the part of Parliament when serious trouble began.
Puritan prejudice against these ' sinful heathenish lewd ungodly
spectacles and most pernicious corruptions' provided a moral
justification for an act of policy. The players, as the abstract
and brief chronicles of the time, were far too dangerous to be
left at liberty to utter what they would to excitable London
audiences during the Civil War.

The fifteen years before the Civil War is not one of the great
epochs of English drama. The veteran Ben Jonson complained
that amateurs were spoiling the stage:

> *Now each Court Hobby horse will wince in rhyme;*
> *Both learned and unlearned, all write plays.*

Shackerley Marmion, a professional playwright of a younger
generation, complained of " this licentious generation of poets "
who troubled the peace of the whole town by turning everything that happened into a play. So that a scrivener could not
lose his ears,

> *Nor a Justice of the Peace share with his clerk,*
> *A lord can't walk drunk with a torch before him,*
> *A gallant can't be suffer'd to pawn's breeches*
> *Or leave his cloak behind him at a tavern,*

but the poets would be writing about it. The chief sinners, in
James Shirley's estimation, were the young university men who

would come up to London 'like market women with dorsers full of lamentable tragedies and ridiculous comedies'.

Certainly, but for the three great plays of John Ford, the 'thirties were not remarkable for poetry on the stage. Both tragedy and pastoral were blown out with wordy pretentiousness and had come to depend too much on over-ingenious intrigues, on magnificent costumes and on scenic effects imitated from the masques.

> *In scene magnificent and language high*
> *And clothes worth all the rest . . .*

complained Richard Brome, thinking perhaps of the insipid works of writers like Ludovic Carlell or the courtier Sir John Suckling's absurd *Aglaura*. But Brome was hardly fair in suggesting that the clique which admired such plays had taught the public to

> *. . . despise all sportive merry wit*
> *Because some such great play has none of it.*

To judge by the number of comedies written, the demand for comedy was as strong as ever. If the public sometimes had a mind to sugared kickshaws and wished to see imaginary Kings, Queens, knights and ladies performing improbable actions, at other times it robustly clamoured for the beef and bag-pudding of topical comedy.

The comedies of this time are not of course purely topical. They share a number of stock situations and stock characters—often frank plagiarisms of Ben Jonson—with the comedies of the two previous generations and some with the comedy of all time. The pert page, the sly waiting woman, the talkative old nurse belong to comedy through the ages. The comic Justice of the Peace, and the stupid constable are peculiar to England, though not to one decade rather than another. Justice Bumpsey, Justice Testy, Justice Cockbrayne are followers in the tradition of Jonson's Overdo and Shakespeare's Shallow. If these gentlemen had fairly represented the average ability of the Justices of the time it would be hard to understand how the administration functioned, more especially if they were seconded by Constables of the line of Dogberry. Constable Busy in *A Match at Midnight* (1633) locks up ' twelve gentlewomen, our own neighbours,' for being in the street after dark on their way to help a friend in labour He will have none of their excuse for going out at night; their friend should have ' cried out at some other time '.

The comic Frenchman—usually a dancing master—the comic Dutchman, drunk and valiant, the comic Welshman, fiery and boastful but good-humoured and brave, were all popular figures. So were the low life characters—the bawds, the cut-purses, the confidence tricksters, and the unemployed soldiers living by their wits. These latter have a long pedigree in English comedy but they became more common in the comedies of the 'thirties just as their prototypes were becoming more common about the streets of London. England stood neutral in the wars of Germany and the Netherlands; and both, or rather all, sides recruited indifferently in the British Isles. The officer from the foreign wars, known by his " taff'ta scarf and long estridge wing " was a familiar figure in the London taverns. The indifference of the professional to the cause which employed him was now and again the subject of comment. Young Palatine in Davenant's *The Wits* (1634) mocks a more scrupulous warrior with

> *What is't to thee, whether one Don Diego*
> *A Prince, or Hans van Holme, fritter seller*

*Of Bombell, do conquer that parapet*
*Redoubt or town, which thou ne'er saw'st before?*

But Justice Cockbrayne, in Brome's *Covent Garden Weeded*, probably overdid the part when he disguised himself as a soldier and boasted: "I have seen the face of war, and serv'd in the Low Countries, though I say't, on both sides."

While the stock types still continued popular in the reign of Charles I, the introduction of some new figures and the development, or the more frequent appearance, of certain older ones, point to the pre-occupations of the time. The decayed gentleman or dispossessed landowner (Dryground, Monylack), the city usurer (Bloodhound, Hornet, Vermin, Quicksands), the feckless courtier living by his wits, the tradesman—and occasionally the yeoman—turned gentleman, the citizen's wife with ambitions beyond her station: all these turn up with almost monotonous regularity.

The comedies do not present an exact picture of what was going on, but by the exaggeration of some elements in the social situation and emphasis on others they clearly reflect the prejudices and anxieties of the audiences who watched them. Wealth was changing hands; the structure of society was being modified by the upward thrust of yeomen and tradesmen into the gentry, while the intelligent gentry consolidated their position by engaging in trade. Examples of this shifting and coalescence of classes are repeatedly given in the comedies of this period, sometimes with a direct, sometimes with only an implied comment. 'I am a gentleman', claims one Startup in Shirley's *Constant Maid* (1640), 'my father was a yeoman, my grandfather was a nobleman's footman.' Sir Paul Squelch the Justice of the Peace in Brome's *Northern Lass*, (1632) is the son of a rich grazier and the grandson of a ploughman. Massinger in *The City Madam* (1632) comments on the invasion of trade by the gentry:

> *masters never prospered*
> *Since gentlemen's sons grew prentices: when we look*
> *To have our business done at home, they are*
> *Abroad in the tennis court.*

But there is one surprising characteristic of the social commentary of this period. The Puritans are let off very lightly. In King James's reign Ben Jonson had dealt ruthlessly with them in *Bartholomew Fair* and in *The Alchemist*. But Zeal-of-the-land Busy, Tribulation Wholesome, and Ananias had few imitators, perhaps because it was felt that no better could be done. During King Charles's personal rule, when the anti-Puritan stage might have been expected to pursue the godly with relentless ridicule, few comic Puritans are to be found. There are references to them of course, allusions to silenced ministers, and to preaching sectaries of both sexes, mockery of their attitude to love-locks, Sunday pastimes and maypoles. But the criticism is on the whole good-natured, and lacks entirely the bitterness and bite of Jonson's attack. In Davenant's *News from Plymouth* (1635), Cable, the sea-captain wooing a widow of Puritan sympathies, tells her

> *I know*
> *You love to frequent the silenc'd parties;*
> *Let but their lungs hold out, and I'll listen*
> *Till my ears ache.*

In case this should not prove his sincerity he gaily adds a promise to cut down his mainmast because it resembles a maypole. In Davenant's *Wits* occurs that description, much quoted by modern economic historians, of the 'weaver of Banbury that hopes to entice Heaven by singing to make him lord of twenty looms'.

Cartwright, himself an Anglican divine, makes the strongest attack on the Puritans in *The Ordinary*, but even this hardly goes beyond the bounds of good nature. In the last scene the gang of rogues who frequent *The Ordinary* from which the play has its name, decide to seek their fortunes in New England. The inhabitants, who have

> one eye
> *Put out with Zeal, th'other with ignorance,*

ought to be easy game. The tricksters will need only to cut their hair to the right length and

> *Nosing a little treason gainst the King,*
> *Bark something at the Bishops,*

and garnish their talk with 'now and then a root or two of Hebrew'.

It is fairly evident from this mild treatment that the public, while ready to laugh at the excesses of fanatics, was no longer in the mood to think Puritan-baiting as funny as it had been twenty years before. The King was doing too much of it and the sympathies of the Londoners were not with him.

The treatment of the Anglican clergy had scarcely altered since Shakespeare's time. The curate appears only as a comic figure or as a necessary convenience to the plot, like Sir Boniface the down-at-heel pedant who marries runaway couples in Heywood's *Wise Woman of Hogsden* (1638). Frequently he has not even a name and appears at the foot of the Dramatis Personæ among servants and supers as *Curate*. When he is given a name it will be something unflattering like Quailpipe, my lord's chaplain in Brome's *The Antipodes*. His wife, when he has one, fares no better. Davenant paints her unkindly

> *Mother Spectacles, the curate's wife*
> *Who does inveigh 'gainst curling and dyed cheeks,*
> *Heaves her devout, impatient nose at oil*
> *Of jesamine, and thinks powder of Paris more*
> *Profane than th'ashes of a Romish martyr.*

Two of the least reputable clergy appear in Cartwright as ' clubbers at the Ordinary '. Sir Christopher, a rather low church divine whose wordy sermons Cartwright parodies in the play, declares bitterly that ' poor labourers in divinity can't earn their groat a day '. His companion, Vicar Catchmey, a " singing man " out of a job, is equally poor and both are represented as hovering in want and bewilderment very near the brink of the criminal underworld.

This attitude to the unfortunate Anglican clergy reflects the popular opinion of the time. Lack of respect for the ministers of the established Church was quite as great a block in the path of Laudian policy as the active opposition of the Puritans.

The religious controversy was a theme too dangerous and too inflammable to be openly touched on by the dramatists. But the social problem, the changes in society, the pretensions of the new rich and the troubles of the new poor were freely discussed. Even the King's financial shifts were treated as the subject of comedy and the sale of titles provided good material for jokes.

In Shirley's *Love in a Maze* (1631) the foolish new-made knight Sir Gervase Simple is contemptuously described:

> *one that has*
> *But newly cast his country skin, come up*
> *To see the fashions of the town, has crept*

> *Into a knighthood, which he paid for heartily,*
> *And, in his best clothes, is suspected*
> *For a gentleman.*

In John Carvell's play, *The Soddered Citizen*, the title buyer is a lord, but

> *He's of our city breed . . . he bought*
> *His raw green honour with the overplus*
> *Of what his father left, of purchasing,*
> *Got in his shop, by 's " What dee lack? " and fawning.*

The great number of the new knights who came into being when the King, to increase his revenues, revived the old knighthood fees, could hardly pass without comment. In Brome's *The Damoiselle* these ordinary knights are compared to cob nuts—

> *He was one of the cob knights in the throng*
> *When they were dubbed in clusters.*

An unpleasant young snob in Shirley's *The Ball* (1632), who can go nowhere without boasting that he is cousin to a lord, shows his mettle by announcing:

> *I care no more for killing half a dozen knights of the*
> *Lower House, I mean that are not descended from nobility,*
> *Than I do to kick my footman.*

Davenant makes use of the royal sale of honours to mock the pretensions of ladies who elevate their chambermaids into " Waiting gentlewomen ". Widow Carrack in *News from Plymouth* tells her maid Smoothall:

> *I may make thee a gentlewoman, though thy mother*
> *Was Goody Smoothall, and do it by my lord's patent*
> *When I am a baroness: 'tis now in fashion*

*To metamorphose chambermaids. The King*
*Dubs knights, and new stamp't honour creates gentry.*

Neither the dramatists nor the audience held the view that
rising in the world, acquiring an estate or buying a title, was
in itself wrong. Worth deserved a material reward and wealth
that had been honestly earned was wholly respectable. In
Brome's *The Damoiselle* a citizen who has acquired gentility by
acquiring land is thus defended against the criticisms of a born,
but impoverished, gentleman:

> *Land lordship's real honour*
> *Though in a tradesman's son: when your fair titles*
> *Are but the shadow of your ancestry:*
> *And you walk in 'em, when your land is gone*
> *Like the pale ghosts of dead nobility.*

But the honest acquisition of wealth as a theme, the success
story of the old Dick Whittington variety, was out of fashion.
On the contrary plays were now more often written on the
theme of successful dishonesty, as in Mayne's *City Wit* or
Davenant's *The Wits.*

Bewildered as they usually were by the operations of capitalism
which surrounded them, the dramatists and the great majority
of the audience were disposed to think that any transaction by
which money was made to multiply, without the labour of the
owner, must be dishonest. Usurers, goldsmiths, lawyers,
scriveners and all such as dealt in loans and mortgages, were
natural villains on the stage.

> *That man who has the readiest way to cheat*
> *Wins all the glory, wealth, esteem, grows great,*

reflects the villainous goldsmith in Carvell's *Soddered Citizen.*

He next enters into an ingenious plot with a friend. They will buy an estate jointly. One of them will then dispose of it to some unsuspecting innocent. After the sale, the other will make his appearance with title deeds showing that the estate was jointly owned and has been sold without his permission. The victim will be forced either to relinquish the estate or to buy him out. In either case there will be proceeds to share.

The most famous of all the blood-suckers is the veteran Massinger's tremendous creation, Sir Giles Overreach, the dark, overshadowing villain of *A New Way to Pay Old Debts* (c. 1623). Beside him, financiers like Brome's Vermin and Shirley's Hornet are mere pygmies. Massinger, whose boldness, force and colour belonged to an earlier generation of dramatists, was a much more violent satirist than the younger men who rose to fame in the sixteen-thirties. Overreach shared his Christian name and some of his characteristics with Sir Giles Mompesson, a financier once greatly favoured at Court, who had been attacked by Parliament and had crashed to ruin in 1621. One of the relatively few references to enclosure occurs in this play, where Overreach is described as ' the grand incloser of what was common '. The younger generation of dramatists tended to write almost exclusively about London, where enclosure was not a topic of the first interest. Massinger and his generation still drew on the whole countryside for their themes, and Overreach is not a city figure, but one of the new financier-landowners who, by fair or foul practices, were building up large estates in the country.

Overreach, like all the successful rich men of the epoch, has to establish his social position and plans to do so by marrying his daughter to a lord. To make certain of this alliance he suggests to the girl that she should lure the lord into a compromising position so that he can be compelled to marry her. The girl's innocence and the lord's shining virtue prevent any such thing happening and Overreach is effectively over-reached in the last act.

The theme of intermarriage between the children of the self-made and the decaying nobility and gentry could be, and was, variously handled. James Shirley, in *The Witty Fair One* (1628) expressed pity for the young women and contempt for those who sought this way of bolstering up their fortunes:

> *not a virgin*
> *Left by her friends heir to a noble fortune*
> *But she's in danger of a marriage*
> *To some puffed title.*

A character in Shackerley Marmion's *A Fine Companion* takes a more severely practical view, " Why, sir, your citizens' widows are the only rubbish (i.e. rubble) of the kingdom, to fill up the breaches of the decayed houses ". Celestina in Shirley's *Lady of Pleasure* (1635), a young rich widow herself, although anxious not to be carried off too soon, has no great aversion to the probable fate which will overtake her, when the court gentleman

> *Claps in with his gilt coach and Flandrian trotters*
> *And hurries her away to be a countess.*

William Davenant, a courtier, regrets the necessity which compels the ' female issue of our decay'd nobility ' to

> *quarter arms with the City*
> *And match with saucy haberdashers' sons.*

The opportunities for comedy afforded by the more innocent and more absurd pretensions of the new rich, and especially their wives, were freely exploited. In Massinger's *City Madam* (1632), the rich citizen's wife has turned her house into a little court. She will have only French or Italian cooks to dress her meat and scorns her poor husband who thinks he has done very well in engaging the Lord Mayor's cook to prepare her a banquet. When three sucking pigs, fattened on muscadine and costing twenty marks apiece, are set on the table she waves them away as not good enough for her. Her husband expostulates with her on her extravagance, reminding her of earlier days when

>                      *you wore*
> *Satin on solemn days, a chain of gold,*
> *A velvet hood, rich borders, and sometimes*
> *A dainty miniver cap, a silver pin*
> *Headed with a pearl worth threepence, and thus far*
> *You were privileged and no man envied it:*
> *It being for the City's honour that*
> *There should be a distinction between*
> *The wife of a patrician and plebian.*

But now with her 'Hungerland bands and Spanish quellio ruffs' his wife will be as fine as a Court lady: she spends forty pounds on a nightgown and when she receives her gossips after lying-in has the baby in a rich canopied crib like a young prince. The dramatists usually saw to it that such proud ladies ended humble and penitent, well content to go back to their miniver caps, velvet hoods and threepenny pearls.

Massinger's *City Madam*, like Chapman and Marston's *Eastward Ho* a generation earlier, developed, with modern trappings, the time-honoured theme of the over-proud woman. But a new element was introduced into the treatment of city wives by the younger generation of dramatists. The citizen's wife is now not merely pretentious, but anxious to show her quality by having a lord for a lover. This was not difficult to manage because the young sparks at the Court were—the dramatists of the 'thirties are wonderfully in agreement on the subject—very willing to seduce a citizen's wife so that they might get their hands into her husband's coffers. The first step was usually to smuggle her into the gallery at a Court masque and make love to her in the dark.

A city beauty of this kind, Alice Saleware, in Brome's *The Mad Couple Well Match'd* (c. 1638), sits in her husband's shop ' more glorious than the Maidenhead in the Mercer's Arms, the Nonpareil, the Paragon of the City, the Flower de Luce of Cheapside . . .' She has several Court admirers and she cleverly persuades her doting husband that if he wishes to appear like a gentleman he must not hang over her all the time or even share a room with her—' that were most uncourtly '. Her plans are, however, brought to nothing by an unexpected turn of events. Her Court lover becomes virtuous.

The reputation of King Charles's Court and of elegant society in general is somewhat ambiguously reflected in these plays. Prynne's attack on the morality of the stage and his supposed reflection on the Queen in *Histriomastix* (1633) caused both Brome and Shirley to come to the defence of their own profession and of the innocent amusements of the Court. Prynne had declared ' delight and skill in dancing a badge of lewd lascivious women and strumpets '. Several of Shirley's plays seem designed to do little else but prove the contrary to be the case, and even Brome, who was far less favourable to the Court than Shirley, introduced a scene into his *Sparagus Garden* (1635), with the sole purpose of defending the reputation of the Court.

Sparagus Garden was an expensive pleasure ground on the south bank of the river, where asparagus and fresh strawberries were served, with sugar and wine, at exorbitant prices. The place had walks, lawns and arbours, and private rooms could be hired in the adjoining eating houses. The Garden had a dubious reputation but was patronized by some of the Court. Brome in his play brings the usual gang of tricksters, gulls and citizens' wives to this resort. They are at once much impressed to see three Court ladies—'Every lady with her own husband: what a virtuous, honest age is this'. Shortly after, the Court party reappears; they engage in dull conversation, and dance a stately measure 'to help digestion'. The dance ended, one lady priggishly cries out that she sees some 'wicked ones' approaching, to which her virtuous gallant replies:

> *May the example of our harmless mirth*
> *And civil recreation purge the place*
> *Of all foul purposes . . .*
> *We seek not to abridge their privilege*
> *Nor can their ill hurt us; we are safe.*

If Brome had depicted any more of the Court's 'harmless mirth' in this style he would soon have brought it into ridicule, but this type of scene—which is apparently intended seriously—does not recur.

Shirley, a more consistent defender of the royal reputation and policy than Brome, offers a well-deserved compliment to the King and Queen in his *Lady of Pleasure*. His heroine, congratulating a courtier-rake on his reform, attributes it to the truth and innocence.

> *which shine*
> *So bright in the two royal luminaries:*
> *At Court you cannot lose your way to chastity.*

This high opinion of the Court was not shared by the Londoners in general. It must be remembered that most of the eulogies of King Charles's Court, with which we are familiar, were written after the King's death when its virtues shone all the more brightly by comparison with the disorders of the exile and the Court of

Charles II. This posthumous reputation makes it difficult to form a dispassionate estimate of the opinion in which contemporaries held it, but comedies, especially Shirley's, throw an interesting light on the question.

Many of these comedies turn on the misinterpretation or slandering of innocence. This is a time-worn theme, but when it was used by the playwrights of an earlier generation the innocent person was almost invariably the victim of a plot—like the unfortunate Hero in *Much Ado*. In plays of the sixteen-thirties on the other hand, the innocent have only themselves to blame: they persistently conduct themselves with an indiscretion that cannot but cause comment, and indulge in the most dubious manœuvres. The young people of *The Ball*, *The Lady of Pleasure*, *Love in a Maze*, all behave with the utmost freedom and pour scorn on the malicious comments of a censorious world.

Celestina, the young widow in *A Lady of Pleasure*, takes a house in the Strand and announces her intention of leading a gay but virtuous life. She encourages admirers and when one of them ventures on a dishonourable proposal she magnificently turns the tables on him in a scene plagiarised from that between Bertram and Diana in *All's Well*. She suggests that he should sell his coat-of-arms and when he indignantly refuses, declares that her honour, like his, cannot be bought and sold:

> *think, think, my lord,*
> *To what you would unworthily betray me,*
> *If you would not, for price of gold or pleasure,*
> *(If that be more your idol) lose the glory*
> *And painted honour of your house.*

In *The Gamester* an unfaithful husband is reformed by being deceived into a belief that his virtuous wife has been unfaithful too. She herself is a cheerfully consenting party to this deception which goes on for several acts. The plot is an adaptation from a story in *The Heptameron*, but Charles I himself seems to have suggested it to Shirley for a play and he was delighted with the way in which Shirley had handled it. In Brome's *The Damoiselle* an impoverished knight advertises a raffle of his daughter and sells tickets at twenty pounds a piece. This unspeakable conduct turns out to be an ingenious trick to collect a dowry for her while making her beauty and innocence shine the brighter.

The theme which emerges from all these complicated intrigues is simply that virtue and innocence are to be judged by the inward intention, not by the outward appearance. This idea was the foundation of the practice of Platonic love which had recently come from France and was fashionable at Court. In Davenant's *Platonic Lovers*, which makes light-hearted fun of the convention, the avowed Platonic lovers, Theander and Eurithea, are allowed to be in each other's company at all hours unchaperoned without giving rise to scandal because they are

> *lovers of a pure*
> *Celestial kind, such as some style Platonical,*
> *A new court epithet scarce understood:*
> *But all they woo, sir, is the spirit, face,*
> *And heart: therefore their conversation is*
> *More safe to fame.*

Platonic love was all very well at Court where the conventions were accepted, but it made a very different impression outside the charmed circle, and the Queen's willingness to be the central star in this whole planetary system of courtly love gave rise to a great deal of groundless gossip and malicious scandal.

On the stage, at least by the conventions of the time, the innocent had only to declare themselves for all slanders to vanish away. In real life it was not so, and the misunderstandings which thickened about King Charles, his Queen and his Court during his personal rule played their part in undermining the position and power of the Crown.

The extravagance of the Court was another cause for complaint. Courtiers were not noted for punctuality in meeting their obligations, and the special privileges which protected them from arrest for debt were very unpopular. A similar privilege, protecting members of Parliament came to be hated no less bitterly after 1640. Davenant set his play *The Unfortunate Lovers* in an imaginary Italy, but the experiences, and the conversation, of the gay young courtier Rampino belong none the less to Whitehall. In the first act, he shows some visitors over the palace, asking them to walk boldly and not slink about or they will be taken for city spies trying to collect debts. Later, when he cannot pay his tailor, Friskin, he offers to get him court preferment, and perhaps a rocker's place to the next young prince or princess for the sempstress to whom he also owes money. The tailor, a man of ambition, is delighted with this and begins at once to boast of the future glories of the House of Friskin.

It was a serious weakness in King Charles and in some of his advisers—notably the Earl of Strafford—not to realize that a bad reputation, however undeserved, and a scandal, however baseless, can be dangerous to the government. They persistently tried to suppress criticism, where they should have removed its causes.

The King, and his father before him, had always striven to prevent their subjects from indulging in " idle talk ", in loose or scandalous speeches. But Charles appears to have believed that the ordinary tendency of human nature to speculate on public affairs, or on the private affairs of public men, could be stifled by stopping up the sources through which the public gained its information. Without news, he calculated, there could be no gossip about public affairs. When criticism of his foreign policy became too vocal, he accordingly prohibited the importation of the foreign news letters, the *corantoes*, out of which his people gleaned their knowledge of what went on in the great world. (With a far clearer understanding of human nature, Cardinal Richelieu at the same time in France took charge of the press and fed it plentifully with such news as he wished the people to have. King Charles only learnt this trick during the Civil War when he began to publish an official newspaper, *Mercurius Aulicus*, at Oxford.)

The prohibition of the *corantoes* and the discouragement of newspapers generally, is several times mentioned in contemporary plays. Lucina, in *The Ball*, declares scornfully that people with nothing better to do will fall back on private scandal " when *corantoes* fail ". Thomas Heywood, in the prologue to *The Late Lancashire Witches* excuses himself for taking up this domestic and local theme, because of the lack of more significant subjects—

> *Corantoes failing, and no foot post late*
> *Possessing us with news of foreign state.*

That the news in the corantoes was inadequate and often false was generally known—Ben Jonson had mocked at them in an earlier generation—but they provided a contact with the outside world, they fed the public interest in the fate of the Protestant Cause in Europe and they were extremely popular. Therefore they continued to be smuggled into the country and were supplemented by handwritten sheets, circulated by enterprising newsmongers. Some of the sources used by these underhand journalists were moderately reliable; most were not. Shirley declared that your professional journalist 'will write you a battle in any part of Europe at an hour's warning, and yet never set foot out of a tavern'.

Davenant devoted the sub-plot in *News from Plymouth* to discrediting the newsmonger. Sir Solomon Trifle, a Justice of the Peace, supplements his income by compiling a newsletter which he distributes through various agents, one of whom is a Puritan called Zeal. When his creatures call on him, he explains his manner of business to a friend:

> *They come for news; man's nature's greedy of it.*
> *We wise men forge it, and the credulous vulgar,*
> *Our instruments, disperse it . . .*
> *News of all sorts and sizes, I have studied hard*
> *And from the general courants and gazettes,*
> *Public and private, letters from all parts*
> *Of Christendom, though they speak contraries,*
> *Weigh'd and reduc'd them to such certainties*
> *That I dare warrant 'em authentical*
> *Under my hand and seal . . .*

His authentical news follows:

> *Rome is taken*
> *By the ships of Amsterdam, and the Pope himself*
> *To save his life turn'd Brownist . . .*
> *. . . The Spanish fleet*
> *That anchor'd off Gibraltar, is sunk*
> *By the French horse . . .*
> *. . . From the Low Countries*

> *Antwerp is plundered, Brussels burnt, the cannon*
> *Brought before Lovaine, and the Prince of Orange*
> *Stands to be Emperor.*

At this point the sceptical listener interrupts:

> *The Emperor lives!*

Not in the least put out, Sir Solomon continues:

> *But is to die the tenth of October next,*
> *And he has it in reversion. From France:*
> *Rochelle recovered by the Huguenots,*
> *And the fifth July last, yes, 'tis the fifth,*
> *The Cardinal Richelieu as he slept in his tent,*
> *Had his head cut off with an invisible sword*
> *By the Great Constable's ghost.*

This monstrous newsmonger is very properly arrested in the last act for holding unlawful intelligence with foreign princes. Less properly, he is threatened with the rack to divulge his sources of information.

James Shirley as well as the courtier playwrights and most of the university amateurs—Davenant, Mayne, Cartwright—supported the royal policies in so far as they mentioned them at all. Massinger and Brome on the other hand could be critical, Massinger sometimes so broadly—as in the case of the King's demands for money mentioned before—that the offending passage had to be deleted. Brome in *The Court Beggar* took up the abuse of monopolies and patents, which was one of the King's most fruitful ways of raising money during his unparliamentary rule. The satire is conceived in general terms and owes a great deal —as Brome usually does—to his master's, Jonson's, treatment of a similar subject in *The Devil is an Asse*. The Parliament of

1624 had made monopolies illegal, but they had crept in again under the transparent disguise of patents. Monopoly rights were granted to those who claimed to have some special process or invention or some interesting experimental scheme for trade or industry. Projects, as they were called, were put forward in great numbers by hangers-on of the Court. In Brome's play a country knight, Sir Andrew Mendicant, comes to London and wastes his fortune trying to procure a grant of this kind. The Court is represented as being surrounded by sharks who will, for a consideration, suggest hopeful schemes to men like Sir Andrew and share the proceeds with him, if he can get a grant to operate them. These " projectors ", who follow Sir Andrew about in a babbling chorus, have plans which they assert will bring in fifty thousand pounds a year to them, twice as much to Sir Andrew, and £64,783 7s. 9d. to the Crown. When one of them is asked to change a shilling for two sixpences he has no ready money about him. This, to an audience who still had the gravest suspicion of all credit transactions, was proof positive that the fellow was a fraud.

Among the projects suggested to Sir Andrew is a monopoly of wig-making in the interests of the nation's health, an imposition of a fourpenny tax on any gallant wearing a new fashion on the first day he puts it on, and the establishment of a floating theatre on barges in the Thames so that the watermen may get back some of the custom recently lost to hackney coachmen and the carriers of sedan chairs.

Brome covered himself for this attack on one aspect of the royal policy by strongly defending another part of it in his play. The King in 1632 had issued a proclamation forbidding country gentlemen to come to London except on business. Sir Andrew Mendicant, who is one of these absentee landlords, is upbraided by his daughter for having abandoned his rural seat:

> *Your aim has been to raise*
> *Your state by court suits, begging as some call it,*
> *And for that course you left your country life*
> *To purchase wit at Court . . .*
> *And for the exchange of a fair mansion house,*
> *Large fruitful fields, rich meadows and sweet pastures,*
> *Well cropped with corn and stocked as well with cattle,*
> *A park well stored with deer too and fish ponds in't,*
> *And all this for a lodging in the Strand . . .*

Shirley, with considerable eloquence, in several comedies depicts the folly of country gentlemen and their wives who waste their fortunes in London. But though he can write persuasively of the pleasures of the countryside, he knew the other side of the question. Lady Bornwell, newly arrived in London with her husband, exclaims

> *I would not*
> *Endure again the country conversation*
> *To be lady of six shires! The men*
> *So near the primitive making they retain*
> *A sense of nothing but the earth; their brains*
> *And barren heads standing as much in want*
> *Of ploughing as their ground. To hear a fellow*
> *Make himself merry and his horse with whistling*
> *Sellenger's Round! To observe with what solemnity*
> *They keep their wakes and throw for pewter candlesticks!*

To leave the boredom of the country was one thing, but there was no need to run to the other extreme, and Lady Bornwell's husband complains with some reason of

> *Your charge of gaudy furniture, and pictures*
> *Of this Italian master and that Dutchman,*

*Your mighty looking glasses, like artillery*
*Brought home on engines . . .*
*Fourscore pound suppers for my lord your kinsman,*
*Banquets for t'other lady aunt and cousins,*
*And perfumes that exceed all: train of servants*
*To stifle us at home, and shew abroad*
*More motley than the French or the Venetian*
*About your coach . . .*
*I could accuse the gaiety of your wardrobe*
*And prodigal embroideries, under which*
*Rich satins, plushes, cloth of silver dare*
*Not show their own complexions . . .*

The lure of the town sometimes reached the rich yeoman. In Brome's *Sparagus Garden* the foolish Tim Hoyden from Ta'anton arrives with 'four hundred pounds, sir, I brought it up to town on purpose to make myself a cleare gentleman of it'. He falls at once into the hands of the decayed knight Moneylack who, under pretence of teaching him the ways of the world, removes most of it. Starvation on what he is assured is court fare, provokes a spirit of rebellion in Hoyden: 'Marry, I feel that I am hungry, and that my shrimp diet and sippings have almost famished me and my purse too; slid, I dare be sworn, as I am almost a gentleman, that every bit and spoonful that I have swallowed these ten days, has cost me ten shillings at least'.

Crosswill, the captious country gentleman in *Covent Garden Weeded*, gets off more lightly. His humour being always to cross everyone, he came up to London because 'the Proclamation of Restraint spurred him on'. But he was very well able to take care of himself when he got there.

The theme of this play is a direct imitation of Ben Jonson's

*Bartholomew Fair*, modernized and made topical by being transferred to the new and much talked of region of Covent Garden.
Cockbrayne, a Middlesex Justice of the Peace, who describes
himself as a near relation of Justice Overdo of *Bartholomew Fair*,
disguises himself and mingles with the inhabitants of Covent
Garden in order to discover and reform their sins. He meets
with much the same adventures and misfortunes as did Justice
Overdo at *Bartholomew Fair*. Brome's play falls behind Jonson's
in every respect, but it has a bustling liveliness and is full of
topical allusions. In the first scene Justice Cockbrayne admires
the new buildings:

> I, marry sir! This is something like! These appear like build-
> ings! Here's architecture expressed indeed! It is a most
> sightly situation and fit for gentry and nobility! . . . Yond
> magnificent piece the Piazzo, will excel that at Venice, by
> hearsay, (I ne'er travelled). A hearty blessing on their brains,
> honours and wealths that are projectors, furtherers and per-
> formers of such great works . . . The Surveyor (whoe'er he
> was) has manifested himself the master of this great Art. How
> he has wedded strength to beauty, state to uniformity, com-
> modiousness with perspicuity. All, all as't should be.

The inhabitants, however, are not all as they should be and
Justice Cockbrayne's expedition among them does little to
improve them. Although the nobility and gentry hastened to
take houses in Covent Garden as soon as it was built, so did the
fashionable ladies of pleasure. Soon the new Covent Garden
rivalled the Strand as the place where richly dressed young
women, alluringly seated on balconies could

*angle up*
*The gay peripatetics of the Court.*

The setting of comedies in recognizable places was obviously an attraction to audiences, especially no doubt to those who either could not afford, or did not like, to venture in such places themselves. From the opening scene of *Covent Garden Weeded* it is clear that the buildings must have been represented on the stage—" these appear like buildings ". No doubt the walks and arbours of *Sparagus Garden* were also fairly well imitated on the stage for that play too, so that citizens who could not afford the prices charged at such a resort could get a very good idea of what it was like for their sixpenny or twelvepenny seat at the theatre.

Shirley attempted great realism in his representation of a race meeting in his play *Hyde Park* (1632). The runners in the foot race—one of whom is called by the name of a famous Irish champion—actually cross the stage twice. Although Shirley could hardly do the same when it came to a horse race, he contrives in the dialogue to give a wonderfully vivid impression of the mounting tension as the race is run. The audience could hear the seventeeth-century equivalent of the cry " They're off! " and listen to the shortening odds shouted by excited gamblers as the race was run. The excitement spreads to a group of ladies in the front of the stage who begin to lay bets among themselves—

> *What odds against my lord !—*
> *Silk stockings—*
> *To a pair of perfum'd gloves? I take it—*
> *Done. I'll have them Spanish scent—*
> *The stockings shall be scarlet. If you choose your scent I'll choose*
>   *my colour.*

Gambling ladies were probably not approved of by the majority of the audience but that would merely add spice to the scene.  Incidentally, Shirley has another gambling lady in his play *The Example* (1634).  The representation and the description of extravagant and fashionable pleasures is a marked feature of these plays which, in taste as well as time, stand midway between the Elizabethan and Restoration drama.  Restoration drama is directed to a society audience which itself indulged in expensive pleasures, took them for granted and needed no explanations.  But the public of the sixteen-thirties was still the mixed public for which Shakespeare had written.  The explanatory character of some of the descriptions in Shirley, Brome, and others suggest that in their time it was a popular function of the theatre to provide the humbler members of this mixed audience with glimpses of a " high life " which was something of a mystery to them and of which they already in some measure disapproved.

Another fashionable craze, more innocent than gambling and racing, which figures in the comedies, was that of collecting.  The serious interest in antiquarianism of the later sixteenth and early seventeenth century had by this time spread to less scholarly enthusiasts, who fell an easy prey to fraudulent pedlars of antiques.  Veterano, in Marmion's *The Antiquary* was such a one, although he begins sensibly enough with the statement that ancient things ' are the registers, the chronicles of the age they were made in, and speak the truth of history better than a hundred of your printed commentaries '.  He talks like a good book but behaves like a fool; on being offered a very dilapidated manuscript he recognizes it at once as one of the lost books of the *Republic* penned by Cicero's own hand.

Cartwright introduces an antiquary into *The Ordinary*.  He has been deeply infected with the current passion for Anglo-Saxon studies and uses such phrases as " I ween" and "Waes hale " in his conversation.  From his lips comes the faked folk rhyme which of recent years has been a popular subject for

poker work in Olde Tea Shoppes, being—who knows?—
perhaps taken for the genuine article.

> *St. Francis and St. Benedight*
> *Blesse this house from wicked wight*
> *From the Nightmare and the Goblin*
> *That is hight good fellow Robin.*
> *Keep it from all evil spirits,*
> *Fayries, Weezels, Rats and Ferrets,*
> *From Curfew time*
> *To the next prime.*

These comedies are light, frivolous, essentially ephemeral
stuff and their charm lies in the incidental intelligence that they
give of the things of everyday life in this period of calm before
the Civil Wars.

Those who lived through that epoch were in later life to
look back on the halcyon days before 1642 with much the same
nostalgia that some now living feel for the legendary time before
1914. The survivors of the Civil Wars, of whatever party,
could not but feel that those lost years, which had in truth been
restless, depressed and rather unhappy, had been infinitely sweet.
In retrospect the inestimable blessing of peace made that whole
epoch bright. 'God Almighty send us a happy end of all our
troubles and peace in this poor kingdom again'; Sir Thomas
Knyvett writing in the midst of the Civil Wars uttered the
prayer that was in the hearts of most honest Englishmen.

Something of this feeling about the interlude before the Civil
War inevitably communicates itself to the historian. That epoch
has the air of heightened peace and stillness which belongs to a
time immediately preceding catastrophe. We know that there
was much amiss, that there was distress and unemployment,
trouble over enclosures, persecution of the Puritans, a bad run

of plague in London and much else to darken those years. But there was also much poetry, much singing, wakes, whitsun ales and harvest festivals, jollity in taverns, learned talk in common rooms; crops ripened and were garnered in peace and the housewife and husbandman need fear no enemies save the weather and the gipsies. Life went on normally from day to day with no more than the ordinary anxieties and pleasures. England was by no means all a sunlit garden but there was a kind of truth in Marvell's poignant cry:

> *Oh thou that dear and happy isle*
> *The garden of the world erewhile*
> *Thou Paradise of the four seas*
> *Which heaven planted us to please . . .*
> *Unhappy! shall we never more*
> *That sweet militia restore,*
> *When gardens only had their towers*
> *And all the garrisons were flowers,*
> *When roses only arms might bear*
> *And men did rosy garlands wear?*

The beauty of these plays is that they fix, in phrase after phrase, the vivid ephemeral details of that time, the ordinary pleasures which became so sweet in retrospect simply because they were ordinary: the holiday expeditions to " the city outleaps ", Islington, Newington, Paddington, Kensington, to eat prunes and cream; the busy bustle of Hyde Park on a summer afternoon with a milkmaid leading round her red cow to offer drinks to the ladies, and the gentlemen sending their pages hurrying to ' Grave Maurice's Head ' for ale; the ' booths and bagpipes upon Banstead downs '—though these we have still; the country bumpkins throwing for pewter candlesticks; the citizen's wife bringing her baby home from nurse with her coach stuffed with hampers of fruit and cheese cakes; the common hangings on the walls, The Prodigal Son and the Story of Joseph; the thumbed copy of Foxe's *Martyrs* on the country gentleman's hall table for his tenantry to read while waiting. Out of the comedies we can hear the long-silenced voices talking of everyday things; laughing at the new portable chairs—' the hand-barrows, what call you 'em?—Sedans ', marvelling at the handsome pocket watches—' you have not a gentleman that's a true gentleman without one '; the worldly ladies shopping in the Dutch shops of the New Exchange; the godly ladies trooping to church each with her prayer-book in its green dimity bag.

Take away the improbable intrigues and the ingenious entanglements, and a whole society with its petty pleasures and preoccupations starts into life from the pages of these comedies. It is their real claim on our remembrance; the best that can be said of them was said by Alexander Brome, writing commendatory verses to the plays of his namesake Richard during the Commonwealth:

*we may be glad*
*To see and think on the happiness we had*

# THE COMMON MAN IN THE
# CIVIL WAR

IT IS a good rule for the enquirer who wants to know about
the people of a past epoch that he should " go on reading
until he hears them talking "—a graphic phrase which I learnt
from Mr. G. M. Young. We do not know an age until we are
at home with its ways of thought and manner of expression,
until we can recognize its essential idiom, the commonplaces of
its daily vocabulary, its special tone of voice.

But whose voices does the historian hear? He may read
widely and wisely in official and unofficial papers; he may
ferret through diaries and newspapers, private letters and public
statements, acts of Parliament, plays, poems, sermons, account
books, wills, laundry lists, inventories—all the multifarious sur-
vivals from his chosen epoch which his single brain can absorb.
After all this, whom does he hear talking? It is obvious that the
loudest and clearest voices will be those of the more articulate
members of society, the well-educated, the well-born, the well-
placed. It is easier to pick up the ideas of the college common
room than of the skittle alley, of the lawyer's study, the squire's
dining room and his lady's parlour, than of the yeoman's fireside,
the alehouse, or the laundry. This is true even of an epoch as
richly documented as the English Civil War. We have a clearer
visual image of the lives and personalities of the rich than of the
poor. Some of their houses still stand, more of them at any

rate than of the cottages of the poor; we can see, sometimes still in use, some of their furniture and hangings. We know their faces and the fashion of their clothes from surviving portraits. We have to reconstruct much more laboriously our picture of the home, the possessions, and the daily life of a labourer—the one or two roomed cottage, the earthen floor, the rough table and stool, the bench fixed to the wall, the spinning wheel and wash tub, the straw palliasse for sleeping, the earthenware pots and leather bottles.

The further we go back in time the more difficult is it to distinguish the voices of ordinary people, and the more do we have to rely on literature (when it exists) to fill in the gaps left in the records. Chaucer, Langland, and Shakespeare can sometimes help us. We can discover the economic conditions in which humbler people lived from their wills and the inventories of their goods, but the sound of their voices reaches the records chiefly when they are in trouble—in collision with the law, or petitioning for relief in time of distress. The impression that we get of the life and fate of the common man in past ages is therefore often more gloomy than it would be if we knew more of his behaviour when he was not in the Courts or on the parish.

The middle years of the seventeenth century are particularly interesting because, in the voluble clash of opinions which was stimulated by the disorders of the Civil War, the voice of the common man becomes for the first time clearly distinguishable. Isolated voices had of course been uplifted before from time to time, but in the war years, the religious fervour which had in part caused the war, and the physical upheaval which accompanied it, gave a release and outlet to enquiring, uneducated minds. The hundreds of pamphlets composed by simple people in the Thomason Collection in the British Museum represent only a very small part of what was going on; for one man who could write a pamphlet there were ten who could stand on a tub and preach to their neighbours and a hundred who could debate ideas, cite Scriptures, and talk politics. For every preacher and self-appointed prophet there must have been hundreds more who exercised their wits in ale-house argument or as they worked at the bench or rested in the fields.

The source of their inspiration was the book that they knew best, the Bible, strongly backed by the book they knew second best, Foxe's *Book of Martyrs*. It is not easy to estimate the degree of literacy among the poor, but working people usually left their young children at the petty school while they were at work, at least until the children were old enough to be helpful. These schools were kept by someone who plied a sedentary trade, often a cobbler, and could overlook the children while he did so, and impart after a fashion the letters of the alphabet to those who wanted to learn. Those who could not read got their Bible by ear, and later, when the pamphlet war was raging, picked up the ideas and arguments set forth in print by hearing them read aloud. Their memories, on the average, would be a great deal better than ours, for few human faculties can have declined more than memory with the spread of books and printing.

It is easy enough to mock at the strange fantasies which uneducated people conjured out of their Biblical studies. Dryden, an Anglican and later a Roman Catholic, expresses at the latter end of the seventeenth century, in his *Religio Laici*, only a sad contempt for these illiterate prophets:

> *The Book thus put in every vulgar hand*
> *Which each presumed he best could understand,*
> *The Common Rule became the Common Prey*
> *And at the mercy of the rabble lay.*

### The Common Man in the Civil War

*The tender page with horny fists was gaul'd*
*And he was gifted most who loudest bawled .*
*The Spirit gave the doctoral degree*
*And every member of the company*
*Was of his trade and of the Bible free . . .*
*This was the fruit the private spirit brought*
*Occasion'd by great zeal and little thought . . .*

Great zeal, certainly, but Dryden is wrong in accusing his humble compatriots of "little thought." They may not have thought very well, having no training, but they thought a great deal, and the crime of most of these prophets in the eyes of the educated and privileged was chiefly that people of their kind were not supposed to think at all, or at least not about such matters as these. King James I had deliberately published the *Book of Sports*, permitting his subjects to play games on Sunday, because if they were not so occupied he feared they would speculate on religion and politics which was not fit for them to do. George Thomason, who put all seventeenth-century scholars in his debt by amassing throughout the Civil War every printed pamphlet on which he could lay hands, frequently writes across the title page of some religious outpouring the statement that the author is "a comfit maker in Bucklersbury," a hay-trusser, a cobbler, or some such; he evidently thought the exercise of such a profession sufficient warrant for putting the views of the writer outside serious consideration. No one was more fierce in condemning these low-born prophets than John Taylor, the Water-poet; he was himself a Thames lighter-man, and had established himself as a favoured eccentric in the 1630's by writing doggerel verses and travellers' tales. The vindictive rage which begins to appear in his writing when hundreds of other uneducated men also set up for authors is comic, but a little saddening.

Much of the preaching and prophesying was, naturally, very silly, often hysterical, sometimes a little mad. In the Thomason Collection there are records of strange hallucinations; a little girl had a vision of angels, about the bigness of turkeys, and with the sweetest faces she ever beheld; a troop of wretched beggars were arrested one of whom claimed to be the Woman Clothed with the Sun and the Princess All Glorious Within. There had always been such aberrations, but they multiplied enormously during and immediately after the War, and while their folly is often distressing, the quantity and quality even of these crazy imaginings suggest the extent to which a new light had broken through into the drab and limited lives of the very poor.

For some, religious speculation was never more than an outlet for splendid imaginings which had hitherto nothing on which to feed, or for an egoism which had been starved in the narrow conditions of ordinary life; but with others religious ideas rapidly acquired a practical and secular tinge. Doctrines from the Bible were held to justify social, economic and political changes. Something of the kind had happened often enough before; the late Dr. Schenk in his excellent book on *The Concern for Social Justice in the Puritan Revolution* showed that many of the Leveller doctrines had a respectable pedigree in medieval religious-political ideas. But never had speculation been so widespread, so imaginative, and so formidable as it was to become in the later 1640's. It is as though the common man, who in earlier centuries had hardly been able to get a word in edgeways, had for a brief interlude come to dominate the scene.

Among the multitude of voices, that of John Lilburne was

certainly the loudest. He was admittedly rather an uncommon common man, since genius is always uncommon, and he certainly possessed genius. He came in fact of very small gentry, and being a younger son was early apprenticed to a trade, but he had a knack of identifying himself with almost every predicament and almost every demand of the common man in the middle years of the century. In his innumerable pamphlets he frequently assumes the part of what we might call the common man, for he is very fond of a title which suggests that he is standing out as a representative of " man " in general, and symbolizing in his person the wrongs and suffering inflicted on him by the hand of government, whether King or Parliament or Corporation. He calls himself—to give a specimen handful from the titles of his works—the Christian Man, the Just Man, the Oppressed Man, the Resolved Man, the Innocent Man, the Upright Man, the Afflicted Man. And indeed, as these titles imply, he packed an immense amount of trouble into a life of little more than forty years.

In the 1630's, before the Civil War, he was in trouble with the King's Star Chamber for distributing unlicensed literature; released by the Long Parliament, he enlisted, was taken prisoner at Brentford, tried for high treason and narrowly escaped hanging at the King's hands; subsequently he was exchanged; distinguished himself in the fighting; was wounded; withdrew from the Parliamentary army because he would not take the Covenant which was imposed after the alliance with the Scots; next he was in trouble for unlicensed printing (he was concerned with a whole series of clandestine printing presses during the Civil War); for libelling the Speaker, for libelling the Earl of Manchester and others; he was constantly in and out of the Tower; trying to reform the government of the City of London, trying to break down the monopoly of the Merchant Adventurers in the wool trade; organizing the outcry in the New Model Army against Parliament; then the mouthpiece of the Leveller movement; constantly up against Cromwell, who he believed had betrayed the cause of liberty for which the war had been fought; twice acquitted to loud popular acclamation; sent into exile, he returned and was shut up by an exasperated government, and in 1655 became a Quaker only a year or two before his death. It is a temptation to anyone discussing the common man in the Great Civil War to let John Lilburne steal the show. But it is not really my intention to say very much about the Levellers with whose republican-egalitarian views he is chiefly associated or to discuss the outburst of democratic theories which marked the end of the Civil War. These things have already had their fair share—and perhaps rather more than their fair share—of attention from historians.

What I want briefly to consider are the facts—or some of them—behind these theories; the hard and humble facts about the lives of ordinary people in the war, and the way in which their practical experience stimulated their ambitions and loosened their tongues. In a necessarily brief and partial summary many of my points may seem very obvious, and yet in the analysis and discussion of history the obvious is often overlooked simply because it *is* obvious. Theories and speculations can exercise a greater charm over students of history than bread-and-butter facts, but the truth, or something approaching the truth, in the reconstruction of the past can only be achieved by the constant association of theories with the facts out of which they must, in great part, grow. This is especially important in the epoch of the Civil War, many of the ideas that it generated are so interesting in themselves that we are tempted to study them in isolation, and so to acquire a misleading perspective of what actually happened.

The Civil War was in many ways a disaster. Three hundred years later we still mourn the destruction it wrought; noble houses like Chipping Campden blown up by the Royalists to prevent its falling into enemy hands; or Basing House razed by the conquerors; majestic Pembroke Castle reduced to a shell; the massive walls of Corfe laboriously and vindictively blasted into fragments; and the cathedrals—the shattered glass at Canterbury, the burnt manuscripts at Winchester, the fury of destruction which swept Hereford, Worcester, Rochester, the siege works which blew the central spire of Lichfield to the skies; the fine silver plate melted down for money, and sometimes not even melted but crudely stamped out into ill-shaped coins. Neither the long term nor the immediate destruction was comparable to what was done at the same time in Germany's Thirty Years War, but it was none the less distressing. The destruction of growing crops, the seizure of live stock and goods, the exactions of the armies in cash and kind were not comparable to those of the much larger and more ruthless armies at that time fighting in Europe, and more especially in Germany; but they were none the less to be deplored and they caused much acute, if temporary, distress.

But there were compensations, and if I appear to emphasize these it is not because I underestimate the suffering caused by the war, but simply because its relieving features have been less frequently considered and are less familiar. I do not mean to preach the soothing doctrine that all was for the best, or the platitudinous one that you will gain on the roundabouts what you lose on the swings. But there was some gain to be had out of the disordered conditions of the war, and the common man, in and out of the armies, had his share of it.

Consider for example the city of Leicester, stormed, taken, and plundered on the night of 31 May 1645 by King Charles's men, so that, as Captain Richard Symonds of the Royal Life Guard informs us, by one in the morning there was " scarce a cottage unplundered." This was extremely unpleasant for the citizens of Leicester, but enjoyable for the King's Welsh infantry who had never before had so much wealth in their pockets. A fortnight later when the Royalist infantry surrendered at Naseby, the Parliamentary soldiers relieved them of what was left of their spoil. This was saddening for the Welsh infantry, but enjoyable for the East Anglians and the Londoners who rifled their waggons and knapsacks.

Plunder is an ugly word, said to have come to England from Germany with General Lesley's troops in the Bishops' War of 1640. I do not condone the practice. But at least in a Civil War the losses by plunder are a little mitigated by the fact that property is changing hands between citizens of the same country. It is not being carried out of the country altogether by conquerors. We should guard against the modern fallacy of assuming that the common man will be nothing but a victim in times of public disaster. In the accounts of the borough of Leicester, for instance, are many small payments to messengers sent out to gather news of what was happening in the neighbourhood: six shillings to a man who rode to Coventry to find out what had happened at Kineton fight, as they called the battle of Edgehill. There was someone six shillings better off for the kind of employment that is much in demand in a war. Such payments are frequent in the parish and town records of the period. Archdeacon West in his delightful and informative book *Rude Forefathers* gives extracts from the accounts of a village constable near Newark. Two shillings and fourpence is paid for repairing some armour; a shilling is paid to carters hired for transport by Prince Rupert, and they are given free beer for the journey as well. These small repeated expenses came heavy on a small village, but carters, blacksmiths, and odd job men were earning more money. If the war checked and hampered some kinds of industry it stimulated other kinds. No doubt it stimulated chiefly the unproductive kinds, but its immediate effect was often to absorb unemployment and to put more money into the ragged pockets of casual labourers.

The war brought anxiety, expense, and loss above all to the yeoman and the petty tradesmen, to those who had worked and saved to maintain their small property and their place in the world. Take for instance a typical inventory of the possessions of such a man at this time, a yeoman in Essex: he possessed a great joined table and eight stools, one little joined table and chair, a cupboard and settle with three boxes on it; two dozen pewter saucers, a salt cellar; two feather beds with curtains and bolsters, besides two trundle beds with blankets, coverlets, and pillows, eight pairs of sheets, ten napkins, and one tablecloth; three brass pots, three brazen candlesticks, one large kettle, and one middling kettle; a horse valued at two pounds; wearing apparel and a purse of money together valued at sixty-two pounds. Such a householder as this was in constant anxiety during the Civil War. He was subject to a weekly assessment imposed for the support of the armies; he was quite likely to have his horse seized or stolen by passing troopers; his household goods might be damaged by soldiers quartered on him, or plundered if they got out of hand, as they very frequently did. Both parties quite shamelessly raised money by driving off grazing cattle and selling it back at a price to its indignant owners. A market of this kind was regularly held in the great quadrangle at Christ Church, Oxford, and there are many other examples.

Resistance and revolt against the soldiers came in the end from farmers, not from the very poor. The clubmen who in 1645 banded themselves together against both parties in the West Country were for the most part yeomen, who found leaders among the local lawyers and clergy. They disappeared when the superior discipline of Parliament's New Model Army put an end to plunder and, temporarily at least, lightened the burden against which they had risen to protest. Self-government and self-help were traditions long established in the English village; though there are plenty of examples of men, women, and children taking refuge in woods and ditches for a night or two while fighting was actually going on in their native place, there was no tragic problem of a permanently displaced and fugitive civilian population. Villagers and citizens stayed in their homes and grimly faced the additional problems that the war brought with it. Many were seriously impoverished, a few utterly ruined. Parish accounts at this time frequently record the giving of alms to families who showed certificates to prove that they had once been in better circumstances but had been ruined by the wars, or to wounded men, or to the widows and children of soldiers. Even allowing for a percentage of forged certificates and hard-luck stories there is evidence enough from all over England that the war years were a time of distress.

But there is another side to this. If the laborious tradesman, or yeoman, or respectable artisan who had built up his little business, or husbanded his acres, looked upon the war with anxiety and dismay, his sons, in whom the sap of life was rising, might feel very differently. Richard Baxter reports censoriously that the villages in his part of the country, near Kidderminster, were much quieter after the King's army had passed through in the early months of the war because all the bad young men were swept into it. Bad they may have been; high-spirited they certainly were, and the army offered, to young men impatient of the narrow horizon within which they had been born, an opportunity to see something more of the world.

If in the Civil War the voice of the common man begins to make itself heard to some purpose in English politics, this is in part because so many of them had, during the war, broken away for the first time from the rigid local and traditional pattern into which they had been born.

The use of modern terms in describing the society of another epoch can be misleading. It is convenient to use the word " class," and hard for anyone born in our century to do without it. Indeed I have used some clumsy circumlocutions in the foregoing pages in order to avoid it. But " class " in our sense is a nineteenth-century word and suggests a society stratified laterally as ours now is. There was, of course, some lateral stratification in the seventeenth century, and there were social groups which can be described as " classes " although they did not use the word themselves. The nobility, the larger gentry, the smaller gentry, merchants, yeomen, and so on down to the landless labourer—such stratification of society certainly existed. But the key-word in the seventeenth-century social pattern is not class but degree, which suggests not the lateral grouping of society that we know, but a pyramidal society rising step-by-step from lowest to highest. That is precisely what existed not only in the wider national sense—the King-Lords-and-Commons of seventeenth-century political theory—but in thousands of smaller regional groups, in town and village, throughout the country. Society was made up of small local communities in which each man had and knew his degree, had certain limited means of rising from one degree to the next, and had moreover certain obligations to those above and below him. The dominating loyalties and interests of Englishmen at this time were not class loyalties and interests, but local loyalties and interests within an accepted hierarchy.

A contemporary writer declared that there were as many wars in England as counties, and the war began with a series of disconnected local clashes between men of influence trying to gain control, either for King or Parliament, of the local reserves of arms. At the very outset of the trouble in January 1642, after the King's unsuccessful attempt to arrest the Five Members, the tenants of John Hampden marched in to Westminster from Buckinghamshire, a thousand strong, offering to live and die for Parliament. The incident has an oddly feudal flavour. All over the country in the early months of the war the relationship of mutual obligation between landowner and tenant, or between the man of influence and the " meaner sort " was what chiefly counted in creating the earliest alignments. Anthony Wood records that in the villages round Thame the lesser gentry and clergy were so much obliged to the Hampdens and the Ingoldsbies that they naturally adopted their politics. The obligation could work the other way: for instance Fairfax attacked Wakefield in the spring of 1643 because he was compelled by the outcry of the poor to secure some Royalist prisoners for purposes of exchange; several hundred of his men had been taken and their womenfolk were making such a clamour for their redemption, and were becoming such a burden on the community since their men had gone, that he had to act. Fairfax was wise to yield to this pressure, or to fulfil this obligation.

Lord Derby, the greatest landowner in Lancashire, can serve as an awful warning of what could happen to a man who failed to fulfil his duties to the common man. After a very brief experience of his methods the respectable young men of the Lancashire villages hastened to enlist in the nearest Parliamentary garrisons in order to avoid being seized on by Lord Derby's officers and compelled to fight without pay and without proper arms. His unpaid troops lived by plunder and he made himself so hated in Lancashire that his defeat at Whalley Abbey in the spring of 1643 has one of the few incidents in the Civil War which resembled a Jacquerie. As soon as the cottagers round about saw that Derby was getting the worst of it, they came surging down the hills armed with scythes and flails to wreak vengeance on his detestable robber bands. The shortcomings of his methods were again visible at Marston Moor when his Lancashire men threw down their arms, crying that they were pressed men and did not want to fight.

An unpopular landowner could be, in this way, disastrous. A popular one on the other hand might create—as some of the Cornish gentry did—an extraordinarily effective local force. But regiments raised by a single magnate tended to have little interest in the war beyond loyalty to their leader; the splendid Cornish infantry went to pieces when Sir Bevil Grenville and four or five other active and popular leaders were killed within a few weeks of each other in the summer of 1643. On the Parliament side, the regiments of Denzil Holles and Lord Brooke fought with great courage in the first campaign of the war, but Holles got tired of fighting and Brooke was killed, whereupon their regiments also disappeared.

The influence of the powerful magnates was important in creating the armies on both sides, but it was by no means the only force at work. Coats, boots, and pay were a powerful incentive at the beginning of the war to the unemployed of London, which had been badly depressed for the last year, still more of East Anglia where the weavers were suffering from a prolonged economic crisis. This explains the ease with which Parliament first put an army in the field and the remarkably poor quality of many of the troops. They joined to get a living and a little amusement; and who shall blame them? They had been having a very bad time in the palmy days of peace. As the army of the Earl of Essex marched across the Midlands, the men broke down park railings, killed the deer, pilfered what they took a fancy to, and broke up the churches (in proof of their godliness). Their officers were mostly too inexperienced, or too much afraid of them, to impose any discipline.

Indeed the extraordinary lack of discipline on both sides is a vivid proof of the rather tense relationship brought about by the war between the common man and his rulers. Both sides badly needed troops; both sides found it hard to keep them regularly paid; and the leaders on each side knew very well that deserters from their ranks would be welcomed by the others. There were, of course, exceptions; soldiers with religious principles who refused to desert their cause—like the Parliamentary prisoners taken at Cirencester, many of whom stood up to a great deal of ill-treatment by the Cavaliers in Oxford rather than agree to serve the King. But in general in the early days of the war the rank and file were not very well-informed as to what it was all about. The Parliamentary garrison at Banbury went over to the King after Edgehill; many of the Royalists captured at Alton in December 1643 re-enlisted with Sir William Waller for Parliament; the parliamentary force which surrendered to Rupert outside Newark in March 1644 was disarmed and given leave to march away, but quite a number preferred to join the conquerors. Consequently generals who wanted to prevent their troops deserting were chary of imposing unpopular discipline.

Fairly severe military regulations were of course issued by both sides, and there were intermittent efforts to put them into force. Men were hanged now and again for plunder as a deterrent to others; but the two great volumes of Prince Rupert's correspondence in the British Museum, and the fairly extensive correspondence of Fairfax, Waller, and other Parliamentarians, as well as the indications in contemporary diaries and memoirs, all convey the impression that the first anxiety of every commander was to keep his troops from deserting at whatever cost. The Earl of Essex wrote a letter of almost apologetic courtesy to call back to their duty the men whom he politely described as having " gone to visit their friends " after Edgehill. A year later, we find the Lord Mayor of London strongly objecting to the search made in the City for the deserters—of whom there were hundreds—from Sir William Waller's army. He said they were better employed pursuing their civilian avocations and he would not answer for the good order of London unless the search was called off—which it was. As late as the spring of 1644 an officer under Fairfax in Yorkshire complained that his men " have disbanded themselves and are following the plough and from thence they will not be drawn." Another difficulty with troops who had strong regional attachments was not merely that they refused to march too far from their villages, but that they put the interests of their wives and children first and insisted on returning home to look after them if enemy troops should happen to be anywhere in the neighbourhood.

All this would seem to suggest that the common man, as common soldier, had a fairly good idea of how to look after himself. There were, of course, some compelled and unwilling men in both armies (more in the King's than in Parliament's) but it would be as grave a mistake to regard the soldiers on both sides as, in general, bullied victims as it would be to think of them as convinced and conscious champions of regal authority or of Parliamentary government.

It was a major problem with these armies to create some feeling of corporate loyalty; and this applied as much to the better kind of volunteers as to the pressed men and those who came in merely for plunder and sustenance. It was shown over and over again that men would fight very bravely out of personal loyalty to a good commander, or out of local pride—to show that Cornish men were better than Devon men, or that the men of Halifax were superior to the men of Leeds. But this kind of feeling evaporated when the commander was withdrawn or when circumstances failed to strike a chord of local pride. On the King's side, Charles himself worked extremely hard to create a personal bond between himself and his army. " Your King is both your cause, your quarrel, and your captain. Come life or death, your King will bear you company," he said to his officers before Edgehill. He was meticulous about attending to his military duties at Oxford, regularly going the rounds in person, and when he was on campaign with his armies on several occasions he marched all day on foot with the infantry, a com- mendable gesture at a time when it was quite usual for infantry officers to ride, leaving their men to slog through the mud. But such personal attachment as Charles could inspire by his actual presence was necessarily limited, and the conception of loyalty to a more or less remote King was not enough to hold an army together; loyalty to individual commanders in the end became one of the chief stumbling blocks in the way of a united Royalist force.

The Parliamentary side might appear at the outset to have much the same difficulties. Cromwell, recruiting in the Fens, called upon the young men to rise for " religion and the laws of the land," but it was said, no doubt with truth, that they really enlisted because they hoped, obscurely, that they would get their Fens again out of the clutches of the enclosers. The surge of determination to defend London when the King marched against it after Edgehill in the autumn of 1642 was essentially an expression of civic indignation; the city, deeply divided in its politics, was brought together by the threat of military conquest. In the following August there seems to be something rather more like a sense of national emergency in the enthusiasm with which the London regiments marched to the relief of beleaguered Gloucester, but here again the printed accounts of that gallant business make it very clear that regional pride was involved: the London apprentices were showing the men of Gloucester what one great city could do for another.

Cromwell said, several years later, that he had seen as early as the battle of Edgehill that what was needed was a change of spirit, and the recruiting of the right kind of men. He was only partly right in this, and what he actually said at the time shows that he subscribed to the general view that the solution of the problem lay in having good officers. "If you choose godly, honest men to be captains," he said, "honest men will follow them," and he was one of the first who had the courage and good sense to offend the social hierarchy by appointing on merit officers of humble origin. Cromwell's success showed that there was something in his theory, but good captains were not enough: more was needed to create the sense of corporate unity in the army and a real and conscious belief in a Cause.

Here the Parliamentarians had for a start an enormous advantage over the Royalists. The chaplains who marched with their armies held varying theological views but as Puritans they all believed in preaching: that is, they believed that the first duty of a minister of God was to establish, by expounding the Scriptures, a contact with, and a hold over, his parish, or his congregation, or in this case, the men in his care. His first duty was not to tag along after the officer-in-command doing any paper-work that was necessary. Many Puritan chaplains did of course act as secretaries, and many Royalist chaplains preached good sermons and were concerned for the moral welfare of the troops. But it is none the less true, from a very early stage in the war, that the tendency of the Royalist chaplains was to devote more of their time to serving the interests of the commanders than to preaching the word of God to the troops. They were moreover handicapped by the fact that the Prayer Book, which they were chiefly fighting to preserve, allows no latitude for extempore prayer. The Parliamentarian chaplain could, if he wished—and he usually did—make his prayers as well as his sermons a constant instruction to the troops. The effect of such preaching and praying in creating a corporate belief in a righteous cause can hardly be overestimated. It was strongly assisted by officers like Cromwell, and Philip Skippon of the London Trained Bands, who had himself composed a small manual of devotion for the use of the troops.

In the autumn and winter of 1644-45 both the King and Parliament reorganized their armies in the interests of greater efficiency. The King's reorganization was a failure because he could not impose any real unity; there was no unity of spirit or understanding on which to build. There were only sectional loyalties. Parliament's reorganization created the famous New Model Army, and unity of counsel and command was successfully imposed because already there was a foundation of unity in spirit and understanding on which to build. The ordinary soldiers of the New Model were in process of becoming a new political entity.

But to turn from the effect of the war on the soldiers to its effect on civilians: their condition certainly does not seem at first sight to be very enviable. I have already pointed out that there were certain advantages in the war—the absorption of unemployment and the creation of additional (if not very productive) work for the casual labourer. But this is not very much to put in the balance against the day-to-day inconveniences, the constant financial pressure and the more occasional heavy suffering which the war imposed on the ordinary man and woman.

A nation-wide system of taxation was gradually created by Parliament. It took two forms: the Excise, a purchase-tax at first imposed on less essential goods but steadily extended, and the weekly assessment. The amount of the assessment was fixed by Parliament for each county, but the County Committees (which were really responsible for local government during the war) fixed the sum to be paid by each region. On top of this weekly burden, the commanders of the armies assigned certain quarters to their troops who collected their support from them in cash or kind. The King's commanders did the same, and when the King summoned the loyalist members of Parliament to Oxford they imitated the financial methods of Westminster, and imposed an Excise and assessment in the King's name. It thus quite frequently happened that regions were alternately paying out to the King or to Parliament, according to which was at the moment in control, but although there was plenty of country that was under disputed authority, especially in the Midlands, it was as far as I know unusual for any village to be paying dues to *both* parties at once. When all the surviving minute books of the various County Committees come to be edited, we shall be able to form a much clearer picture of what actually went on during those difficult years. Those that have been examined reveal (in spite of a certain amount of vindictive personal squabbling between the gentry of both parties) a surprising degree of fairness in assessment and competence in collection.

Apart from these hard but regulated exactions, the common

man in the small towns, villages, or open country was subject to a good deal of casual annoyance and plunder. The Cavaliers (and for anything I know to the contrary the Parliamentarians as well) in the early days made a practice of " sweeping the commons " for horses—in other words driving off any horses that people had been foolish enough to put out to grass on the common land. Sir Ralph Hopton, as he advanced from Cornwall in the spring of 1643, took advantage of a market-day to raid Totnes and drive off all the horses he found in the town. In the critical time when the King was advancing on London in the autumn of 1642 the Parliamentarians, being very short of waggons and draught-horses, waylaid the carriers on the roads into London and commandeered their carts. The problem of feeding an army on the march was always difficult, and it was quite usual for the men to drive off cattle and sheep to supply their wants; the soldiers of Essex, as they approached Newbury in the wet autumn of 1643, were driving about a thousand sheep.

The ballads of the day reflect the resentment of pillaged farmers and over-taxed citizens; one of them puts into the mouth of a Parliamentary tyrant the reflection:

> Oh we shall have, if we go on
> In Plunder, Excise and Blood
> But few folks, and poor, to domineer o'er
> And that will not be good.

But a London barrister called Greene whose brief diary jottings have survived makes a reflection which, in our times as well, the ordinary citizen has sometimes discovered to be true: " We begin now to see," he writes, " that a Kingdom according to human discourse is not so easily ruinated and will commonly hold by stronger roots than we imagined; we may hold out, if

God has not determined otherwise, two or three years longer at this rate—only grow poorer and poorer."

He wrote this in the winter of 1642-43; the first Civil War lasted another three and a half years; the assessments continued until the Restoration, and the system of taxation which John Pym and his party initiated—apologetically and with great assertions that it was a temporary measure only—was the beginning of regular national taxation in the modern manner.

But there were mitigating elements in all this, elements which writers of popular ballads, or men and women petitioning against oppression, or seeking to have their assessments reduced, naturally did not emphasize. England was not, to either party, an enemy country; politically it was the aim of Parliament and of the King not to crush or conquer but to win the confidence of the people. Each side emphasized in its propaganda that law and order reigned in the regions it controlled, that citizens would not be plundered and farmers could attend the weekly markets without fear. These statements were not true, but they represented a genuine intention. Quite apart from the political aspects of the matter, neither money nor food for the troops would be forthcoming unless the life of the country was allowed to proceed as far as possible in a normal manner. The King for instance wanted to cut off the trade of London, and he was fairly successful in blocking the roads from London to the West with his great outposts at Donnington Castle and Basing House, but he could not effectively prohibit trade to London until he had an alternative outlet to offer to merchants. This occurred when Prince Rupert took Bristol in July 1643, and the King's attempt to build up Bristol as a rival to London is an interesting side-issue to the war.

Royalist recruiting in North Wales and the fighting in the North Welsh marches very seriously disturbed the cattle-droving on which the economy of the country depended; it also interrupted the Shrewsbury wool trade and turned Shrewsbury in two years from a relatively loyal and friendly into an extremely hostile town, whose citizens in February 1645 joined with the attacking Parliamentary force to capture, kill, or drive out the Royalist garrison. It was naturally the aim of both parties to avoid this kind of thing. Sir Thomas Fairfax, in the West Riding of Yorkshire, made enormous, though unsuccessful, efforts to gain control of the whole region of the four great wool towns, Wakefield, Bradford, Leeds and Halifax, because so long as the Royalists held one half of the West Riding and the Parliamentarians the other, the natural economy of the region was fatally choked, and it became very difficult for either party to draw sustenance from it.

It is therefore true to say that both sides were acutely conscious of the need to preserve the economic life of the country, and on the County Committees soldiers and civilians consulted together in what they hoped would be the best interests of both.

Commanders found it extremely difficult to maintain discipline and prevent the troops from plundering, but there is a great difference between the effects of casual plunder and a deliberate " scorched earth " policy. In the war in Scotland both Montrose and Argyle deliberately laid waste the country of the opposite party, but in England there were no such clear divisions and the deliberate wasting of country in order to prevent the enemy occupying it hardly occurs at all. On the contrary both sides as far as possible tried to prevent the destruction of young corn and fruit-bearing trees. Parliament was unfortunately driven to be reckless about timber because Newcastle was Royalist and therefore had to be blockaded to prevent the King raising money by the sale of coal. London was therefore completely cut off from its normal coal supply and had somehow (and very inadequately) to be provided with fuel by felling trees for thirty miles round, beginning with those in the royal park at Windsor.

There was one other important mitigating factor in the Civil War. The troops, with very few exceptions, were English; they were not alien to the civilian population. The armies did not have time to become professionalized; they were still, up to the end of the war, essentially citizens in arms. There was therefore no irreconcilable hostility between them and the civilian population. They were not, as the professional armies abroad were, an entirely separate order of people at natural enmity with the peasant and the tradesman. We know from contemporary European literature and pictures, from the works of Grimmelshausen, the paintings of Wouwermans, the engravings of Callot and Stefano della Bella, as well as from direct documentary evidence, how furious and how bitter was the division between the professional soldiers and the peasantry on whom they had to live, and whom they regarded as natural victims.

There was nothing, or very little, to be compared with this in England. Naturally a good deal was made of the indiscipline of the troops by the propagandists of the opposite party, but it was in fact ridiculous to compare the brief and more or less accidental plunder and burning at Brentford or Birmingham with the deliberate sacking of Magdeburg and Prague. Occasionally non-combatants were killed defending their goods from plunder, or during the capture of a town, but this was exceptional and was usually deplored by the commander responsible; or if he did not deplore it he would find it necessary to explain that he had, for one reason or another, absolutely no choice in the matter. The accidental killing of civilians was never taken for granted.

When all the mitigating circumstances have been considered, the war can only be thought of as a time of suffering, anxiety, and loss for the majority of the population, at least in their physical and economic condition. It was, as Hugh Peters in a sermon vividly expressed it, a " blessed change . . . to see the highways occupied again; to hear the carter whistling to his toiling team; to see the weekly carrier attend his constant mart; to see the hills rejoicing, the valleys laughing." But the very troubles and disorders through which the country had passed had created the mental and moral atmosphere favourable to changes and questionings more disturbing than the physical distresses through which they had come.

The war had begun in 1642 as a constitutional struggle between King and Parliament—that is, between the King and what was in effect the ruling class. Both parties believed, sincerely enough, in governing for the good of the people, but neither had any idea of giving the people any say in the government. Five years later, in 1647, there came the violent collision between " the people "—or the New Model Army calling itself not unjustly " the people "—and the *Grandees*, the men of property, the triumphant commanders and Parliament men who had originally challenged the King.

This was the obvious outcome of the war. In the last five years great numbers of ordinary Englishmen had seen a world outside their town or village and learnt to think in larger terms of a nation, or a people, as a whole. They had also been encouraged to act in a manner wholly foreign to the rigid social code of their time. In the heat of action they were as likely to see the gentry at a disadvantage as at an advantage. They had fired on their betters, pulled them off their horses, seen them in the ugly humiliations of pain and fear and defeat—the Marquess of Worcester without hat or cloak, helplessly watching the soldiers tear his possessions in pieces, the officers of the defeated garrisons and their wives going out with saddened, straightened faces between the lines of their conquerors. Those who had seen such things might well reflect on how the great were brought low. The war was not six months old when one of the Parliamentary captains (it was young Hotham, later to be executed for treachery) predicted that " the necessitous people," having once learnt the joys and advantages of soldiering, would not hesitate to " cast the rider " and " run like wildfire through all the counties of England." They did not in the end succeed in " casting the rider," but some of them certainly tried.

They had no doubt made other experiences as well. Young men who had never seen anything but, at best, the parlour of some small squire's house, now entered as conquerors some of the greatest houses in England, stared with wonder, or envy, or austere disapproval at the stately splendours of Welbeck, or Bolsover, or Raglan Castle, or Latham House. Disapproval was, I imagine, more frequent with them than envy; there is relatively little trace of vindictiveness of the poor against the rich in anything they said or did. But they had gained a new experience and a new perspective; they had learnt that, in time of war, Jack was as good as his master, and sometimes better.

The egalitarian political theories which spread at the end of the war among the soldiers of the New Model Army were the creation of men with intense and logical ways of thinking, and they had a pedigree that ran back to the Middle Ages. There is nothing startlingly original in the basic claim that all men are equal. But the fervent plea of John Lilburne for the under-privileged and the rapidly spreading doctrines of the Levellers were received with enthusiasm and intelligence because the common man, or common soldier, had in the last five years crossed frontiers of space and of experience which led him to understand that there were interests which united men from Yorkshire, from Staffordshire, from Essex, indeed from all the counties of England. He had learnt to question the authority of the great and to believe in his own capacity. It was one of the great, though accidental, achievements of the English Civil War that it gave the common man a chance, briefly, to taste the possibility of power and to speak his mind.

# CAPTAIN HIND THE HIGHWAYMAN

THERE WAS a noisy arrest one November morning in 1651 at a barber's shop opposite St. Dunstan's Church in Fleet Street. The news spread quickly through the neighbouring alleys so that Captain Hind the Highwayman had a large public when he was brought out, manacled, thrust into a waiting coach and carried off to the Council of State at Westminster. Highwaymen did not, as a rule, command the attention of the Government and I like to think that the dapper little man, as he entered on the last phase of his notorious career, had the gratification of knowing that he had achieved something.

The highwayman proper, as distinguished from the ordinary robber, foot-pad and the other minions of the moon known to Shakespeare, was new to the annals of English crime. The word itself, significantly, begins to occur only during the general relaxation of law and order which accompanied the outbreak of the Civil War in 1642. The armed horseman whose method was to force the wealthy traveller at the pistol's point to hand over his money was perhaps a natural outcome of that time. The highwayman needed steady nerves, firearms and a good horse, all things which a deserter, or a cashiered officer, might very well possess. Highwaymen were not, however, all of this class; indeed relatively few of them were, but the new technique which rapidly became as popular as it was effective was probably learnt from pioneers who had once been soldiers. Sometimes they operated alone, more often in gangs. Many, if not all of them, pretended to a sort of Robinhoodishness. The only prey worth their while were the rich but they made a kind of virtue of this necessity and for that reason, perhaps, were popular, in theory at least, among the poor.

James Hind was one of the first to mark the profession with the strong imprint of his character. His gaiety, his daring, his Royalist sympathies and elegant manners were the familiar talk of inn-keepers and ostlers on every main road. He had ' pranced the road ' from London to York, was well known to Gloucester-shire, the Fens and the Thames valley and had, with his gang, at one time, levied almost regular tribute on the travellers who came to London by way of Barnet Heath.

Fame is not healthy for a highwayman and after a few years Hind fled the country, lurked in the Netherlands, dodged across Ireland and arrived in Scotland just in time to be presented to the young Charles II—who had a weakness for clever scoundrels —and to enlist in the Royalist army as it set out to invade England. He saw action at Warrington and Worcester and after the King's defeat went to earth in the rabbit warren of London's most disreputable quarter.

Hind had ridden as a trooper in the King's army, but his public would not believe that their hero had played so small a part. It was widely rumoured that he had been Scoutmaster General and, when the young King eluded the pursuit of his enemies, it was to the skill and daring of Jemmy Hind that popular opinion attributed his escape.

The flattering rumour was Hind's undoing. Because they thought he might lead them to the King, the Government spared no pains in tracking him down. It was not Captain Hind the Highwayman but James Hind the Royalist whom the Council of State wished to see. The fugitive trooper from the King's defeated army would have been safe enough in London had he not trailed with him into his new profession those tell-tale clouds of glory from his past. His interview with the Council of State was a disappointment to both parties; he turned out to be of no importance to them at all.

Yet it hardly seemed sensible to release a public hero who had also been, in his time, a fairly considerable public nuisance. Direct evidence of his robberies was hard to come by, so he made his appearance at the Old Bailey about a month later on a charge of high treason.

Jemmy Hind was small and personable, with a confidence that did not overflow into swagger and gave him the easy air of a gentleman. A large audience had come to see and hear, hoping for some of his famous jests. The hearing, however, gave him few favourable openings for his wit and it was only at the end that he raised a laugh. Squinting down at his heels as he left the dock—'A plague on these great jingling spurs!' he said, and gave his irons a shake. Outside the crowd pressed upon him with lugubrious sympathy, asking him if he was to be hanged. 'No, no, good people,' he said, 'they are not in such a hurry to hang true folk.'

The fact was that they were not in such a hurry to hang a common thief on the distinguished charge of high treason. Evidence had come to light that, during his operations in Berkshire, he had once killed a man in a brawl; he was transferred to Reading and the charge was altered to manslaughter.

Under a medieval statute not yet repealed it was possible for any man who could read to avoid hanging for manslaughter by pleading benefit of clergy; this reduced the penalty to a formal branding in the palm of the hand. Captain Hind in the dock at Reading was the same civil, witty, confident gentleman that he had been in London. But he had not realised that he would have to prove his right to benefit of clergy. He was utterly taken aback when a book was handed to him and he was told to read a paragraph. The gallant, play-actor's mask of gentility fell from his face: he could not read a word.

It was an eccentricity almost, for even in the humbler class from which he came, illiteracy was unusual. His father was an honest saddler of Chipping Norton who had wanted to make a scholar of his son; Hind had been two years at school but his incorrigible 'waggishness' had prevented him from learning anything at all. Later he had been apprenticed to his father, and, when that did not please him, to a butcher; at the age of about eighteen he borrowed forty shillings from his doting mother and ran away to London.

Here he had fallen in with Allan, the boldest highwayman of his day, who used to disguise himself as a bishop, bowling along in his coach with outriders and servants. Once on a lonely stretch of road, off came the episcopal disguise, the coach was hidden behind a hedge and the gang took up their action stations. When, a little later, the bishop and his train reached the next town, they would listen with sympathy to the story of the robber band which had held up so many travellers that day and thank Heaven that the rogues had not molested them.

Young Hind learnt his profession and his good manners as gentleman usher to Bishop Allan and when Allan 'went to heaven in a piece of string' he set up on his own. The country was still disordered with echoes of civil war. Hind—one of the first gentlemen of the road to do so—adopted the title of Captain and permitted a general belief that he had served in that capacity for the King. His political views were, however, genuine; he robbed Parliament men for preference and once, when he had robbed a poor Cavalier in error, he not only gave him his money back, but dined with him at the next inn on the road, riding off at first light after paying the reckoning for them both. This was an act at once delicate and generous; Hind was a rogue but he was nature's gentleman.

There had been traces of grace and gallantry on the roads before Hind's time, but he was the first who made it a prevailing fashion. He never robbed without a jest and he always, with a little flourish, handed back to his victim a few shillings expenses money for the rest of his journey. In return he expected courtesy from his clients and when a traveller, for whom he had laid an ambush, came dawdling up at a foot pace, he whacked him smartly with his cane and cried ' Have I nothing to do all day but wait for you? '

His quick wits and resourcefulness gave rise to hundreds of tales. When he nipped a bag of gold out of a gentleman's coach at Hyde Park races, he got his booty safely through the London suburbs by waving it in the air as he galloped past, shouting, ' I've won my wager; I've won my wager.' The crowds made way for the jubilant victor and long before the pursuit came up with him, he had vanished.

Another time, when some of his victims were pelting along a dark highway after him, he ran into a happy, drunk parson, coming home from a wedding. Hind pressed his loaded pistol into his hand, breathlessly explaining that highwaymen were after him. Fire, he told the parson, and they'll away. The parson fired wildly, the pursuers took him for their robber, overpowered him and carried him off to prison, while Hind was already safe in the woods. The parson was, of course, a vile Puritan inter-loper; Hind the Cavalier would not have played such a prank on a priest of the Anglican church.

True or false, the stories sprang from a genuine personality— the gay, civil gentleman who, in the dock at Reading, crumpled so pathetically into the saddler's truant son.

But his life was to end more nobly. While he waited for the hanging, Parliament passed an act of oblivion to cover crimes of violence committed during this disorderly epoch of the war. Hind was reprieved. But the authorities would not let so dangerous a thief escape. They revived the charge of high treason and transferred him from Reading gaol to Worcester. Here at the next assizes he was tried and sentenced to be hanged for taking up arms for the usurper Charles Stuart. So, at last, on September 24th, 1652, Jemmy Hind the saddler's son joined the distinguished band of martyrs, knights, esquires and peers of the realm who had mounted the scaffold for their King. He died if not exactly the death of a gentleman, yet a death that many gentleman had not been ashamed to die.